# Keto Bread Cookbook for Family

*The Best Low-carb Breads For You To Enjoy Baking And Eating*

**By**

**Alessandro Vasquez**

# Table of Contents

## The Complete Ketogenic Guidebook for Women Over 50

## Intermittent Fasting for Women Over 50

## The Healthy Keto Meal Prep Cookbook with Pictures

## The 15-Day Keto Fasting Cookbook

## Keto diet Cookbook

# The Complete Ketogenic Guidebook for Women Over 50

*Easy Anti-inflammatory Recipes to Lose Belly Fat, Boost your Metabolism, and increase your energy above the age of 50*

## By

## Alessandro Vasquez

# Table of Contents

# Introduction

A Keto diet is one that is very low in carbohydrates but rich in fats and is normal on protein. Through the years, the Keto diet has been used to treat a variety of diseases that people have learned to face. This includes: rectifying weight gain as well as managing or treating diseases of human beings like treating epilepsy in youngsters. The Keto diet enables the human body to use its fats instead of consuming its carbohydrates. Typically, the body's carbohydrates, which are present in the foods you eat, are transformed into glucose. Glucose is a consequence of the body burning off its carbohydrates which are typically distributed throughout the body. A dietary strategy and a balanced lifestyle are, thus, an important necessity for all the citizens who choose to prevent early mortality. Health problems are widely prevalent in women over the age of 50 since they suffer from normal bodily adjustments related to menopause.

Osteoporosis, hypertension, high blood pressure, overweight, and inflammation are popular among women of this category. An effective metabolism is a secret to good health! The level of metabolism does not stay the same, though! As an individual age, the body naturally moves through a slow metabolic phase. This phase of aging speeds up as we eat unhealthy food and live an unhealthy lifestyle, resulting in a variety of metabolic disorders and other associated diseases. It's a popular myth that you'll be consuming bland and fatty food while you're on a ketogenic diet. Although basic foods are a necessity, there are so many ways to bring the spice back into your diet.

Doing keto doesn't just include consuming any type of fat or having ice cream on the mouth. Instead, it's about choosing products that are high in healthy fats and poor in carbohydrates cautiously. If you aren't sure where to go, don't be afraid. Some really good, fantastic keto meals are out there promising to be eaten.

# Chapter 1: Introduction to Ketogenic Diet

A ketogenic diet is widely known as a diet which is low in carbs and in which the human body generates ketones to be processed as energy in the liver. Several different names are related to a keto diet, lower-carb diet, lower-carb high fat (LCHF), etc. Patterns of diet come and go, and it seems like the formula mostly includes a low-carb plan. At the top of the chart right now is the ketogenic diet. The keto diet, also referred to as the ketogenic diet, relies on having more of the calories from protein and a few from fat while eliminating carbohydrates dramatically.

## 1.1 How Does The Ketogenic Diet Work?

A high fat, medium protein, low carbohydrate diet plan, which varies from standard, balanced eating recommendations, is the ketogenic diet. Many foods abundant in nutrients, including vegetables, fruits, whole grains, milk products, are sources of carbohydrates. Carbs from both types are highly constrained on a keto diet. Keto dieters, therefore, do not eat bread, grains, or cereals with the intention of holding carbs below 50 g a day. And since them, too, contain carbohydrates, even fruits and vegetables are restricted. The keto diet involves making drastic changes about how they normally consume for most individuals.

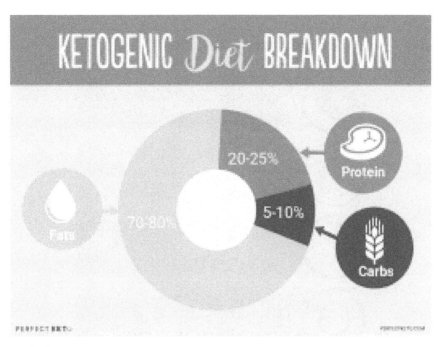

## What is Ketosis?

Ketosis is a metabolic condition where the body utilizes fat and ketones as the main source of fuel instead of glucose (sugar).

A critical part of beginning a keto diet is knowing how Ketosis works. Ketosis, irrespective of the number of carbohydrates you consume, is a phase that the body goes through on a daily basis. This is because if sugar is not readily accessible, this method provides humans energy from ketones.

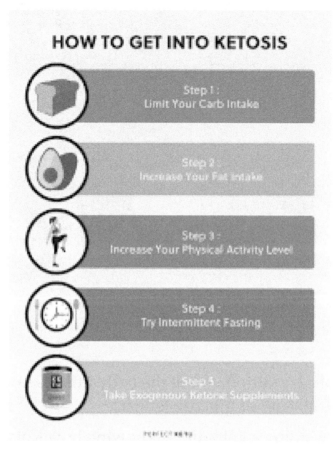

The body tends to raise its ketone levels if the requirement for energy grows, and carbohydrates are not sufficient to satisfy the need. If a more extended period of time (i.e., more than three days) is limited to carbohydrates, the body can raise ketone levels much more. These deeper ketosis rates produce several favorable benefits in the body, results that are achieved when adopting the ketogenic diet is the best and healthiest manner practicable.

Most individuals, however, seldom get Ketosis and never feel its advantages because the body tends to use sugar as its main source of power, even if the diet provides plenty of carbohydrates and protein.

## How does Ketosis happen?

The body would turn any of its accumulated fat into extremely effective energy molecules called ketones while the body has no access to healthy food, like while you are resting, exercising, or adopting a ketogenic diet. (We should credit our body's capacity to alter metabolic processes for that.) After the body breaks down fat into glycerol and fatty acids, such ketones are synthesized.

While in certain cells in the body, fatty acids and glycerol may be directly converted into food, brain cells do not use them as energy at all. This really is because they are so gradually processed into energy to help the brain work.

That's why sugar appears to be the brain's primary source of fuel. Interestingly, this also enables one to realize that we make ketones. Thus providing an alternate source of energy, because we do not eat sufficient calories, our brain will be incredibly susceptible. Our muscles will be quickly broken down and transformed into glucose to support our brains that are sugar-hungry before we have enough power left to find food. The human species would most definitely be endangered without ketones.

## 1.2 Types of Ketogenic Diet

There are a variety of aspects in which ketosis can be induced, and so there are a number of diverse ketogenic diet variations.

**Keto Diet Standard (SKD)**

This is a really low carb diet, a medium protein diet yet high fat. Usually, it comprises 70 to 75% fat, 20% protein, and only 5 to 10% carbohydrates.

A traditional standard ketogenic diet, in terms of grams per day, will be:

- Carbohydrate between 20-50g
- Around 40-60g of protein
- No limit specified for fat

The bulk of calories should be given by fat in the diet for this to be a keto diet. As energy needs might differ greatly among individuals, no limit is set. A large number of vegetables, especially non-starchy veggies, should be included in ketogenic diets, as they are very low in carbs.

In order to help people reduce weight, increase blood glucose regulation and improve cardiac health, standardized ketogenic diets have repeatedly demonstrated success.

## Very-low-carb diet ketogenic (VLCKD)

Very-low-carb is a traditional ketogenic diet, and so a VLCKD would normally correspond to a traditional ketogenic diet.

## Ketogenic Diet Well Formulated (WFKD)

The word 'Well Formulated Keto Diet' derives from one of the main ketogenic diet experts, Steve Phinney.

As a traditional ketogenic diet, the WFKD maintains a similar blueprint. Well-developed ensures that weight, protein & carbohydrate macronutrients align with the ratios of the traditional ketogenic diet and thus have the greatest likelihood of ketosis happening.

## Ketogenic Diet MCT

This fits the description of the traditional ketogenic diet but insists on providing more of the diet's fat content through the use of medium-chain triglycerides (MCTs). MCTs are present in coconut oil and are accessible in the liquid state of MCT oil and MCT dispersant.

To treat epilepsy, MCT ketogenic diets are being used since the idea is that MCTs enable individuals to absorb more carbohydrates and protein, thus sustaining ketosis. That's because multiple ketones per gram of fat are produced by MCTs than the long-chain triglycerides found in natural dietary fat. There is a dearth of research, though, exploring whether MCTs have greater advantages on weight loss and blood sugar.

## Ketogenic diet Calorie-restricted

Unless calories are reduced to a fixed number, a calorie-restricted ketogenic diet is identical to a normal ketogenic diet.

Research indicates that, whether calorie consumption is reduced or not, ketogenic diets seem to be effective. This is because it helps to avoid over-eating of itself from the nutritious impact of eating fat and staying in ketosis.

## The Ketogenic Cyclical Diet (CKD)

There are days on which more carbohydrates are ingested, like five ketogenic days accompanied by two high carbohydrate days, in the CKD diet, frequently recognized as carb back loading.

The diet is meant for athletes who can regenerate glycogen drained from muscles during exercises using the high carbohydrate days.

## Ketogenic Diet Targeted (TKD)

Even though carbs are eaten around exercise hours, the TKD is equivalent to a typical ketogenic diet. It is a combination between a regular ketogenic diet as well as a cyclical ketogenic diet that requires every day you work out to eat carbohydrates.

It is focused on the assumption that carbohydrates eaten before or during a physical effort can be absorbed even more effectively, while the need for energy from the muscles rises while we are engaged.

## Ketogenic Diet of High Protein

With a proportion of 35 percent protein, 60 percent fat, and 5 percent carbohydrates, this diet contains more protein than a regular keto diet.

For people who need to lose weight, a study shows that a high-protein keto is beneficial for weight loss. Like in other types of the ketogenic diet, if practiced for several years, there is an absence of research on which there are any health risks.

## 1.3 Benefits of Ketogenic Diet

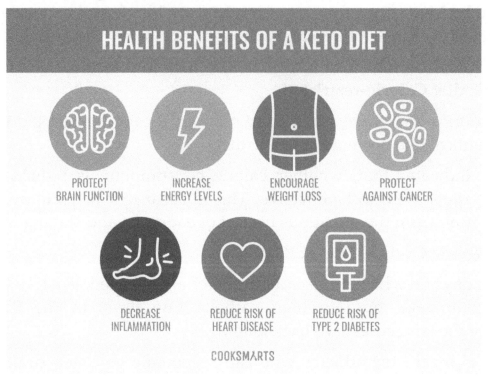

A keto diet has many advantages, including:

## Weight Reduction

A person's keto diet will help them lose weight. The keto diet help encourages weight loss in many aspects, particularly metabolism boosting and appetite reduction. Ketogenic diets comprise foods that load up an individual and can minimize hormones that trigger appetite. For these factors, it may suppress appetite and encourage weight loss by adopting a keto diet.

## Helps improve acne

In certain persons, acne has many common reasons and can have associations with diet and blood sugar. Consuming a diet rich in highly processed carbs can change the equivalence of intestinal bacteria and cause major rises and declines in blood sugar, both of which would negatively impact the health of the skin.

**It can decrease the risk of certain cancers**.

The implications of the ketogenic diet have been studied by experts to potentially avoid or even cure some cancers. One research showed that in patients with some cancers, a ketogenic diet could be a healthy and appropriate complementary medication to be used in addition to chemotherapy and radiation therapy. This is because, in cancer cells, it might cause greater oxidative stress than in regular cells, allowing them to die.

**It can safeguard brain function**.

Some research indicates that neuroprotective advantages are offered by the ketones developed during the ketogenic diet that indicates they can reinforce and defend the brain and nerve cells.

A ketogenic diet might help a person resist or maintain problems such as Alzheimer's disease for this purpose.

**Lessens seizures potentially**

In a ketogenic diet, the proportion of fat, protein, and carbohydrates changes the way the body utilizes energy, results in ketosis. Ketosis is a biochemical mechanism in which ketone bodies are being used by the body for energy.

The Epilepsy Foundation indicates that ketosis in people with epilepsy, particularly those who have not adapted to other types of treatment, might decrease seizures. More study is required on how efficient this is, as it seems to have the greatest influence on children who have generalized seizures.

**Improves the effects of PCOS**

Polycystic ovary syndrome (PCOS) may contribute to surplus male hormones, ovulatory instability, and polycystic ovaries as a hormonal syndrome. In individuals with PCOS, a high-carbohydrate diet can trigger negative impacts, like skin problems as well as excess weight.

The researchers observed that many markers of PCOS are strengthened by a ketogenic diet, including:

- Loss in weight
- Balance of hormones
- Ratios of follicle-stimulating hormone (LH) and luteinizing hormone (LH) (FSH)

- Insulin fasting levels

A different research analysis showed that for people with hormonal conditions, like PCOS and type 2 diabetes, a keto diet has positive benefits. They also cautioned, though, that the findings were too diverse to prescribe a keto diet as a specific PCOS treatment.

## Chapter 2: Easy ketogenic Low Carb Recipes

It may be challenging to adopt different diets: all the foods to quit, to consume more, to purchase new products. It's enough to make bonkers for everyone. But the ketogenic, or "keto," diet, as well as its keto meals, are one type of eating that has been gathering traction lately.

Doing keto doesn't only involve eating some sort of fat or putting ice cream on your mouth. Rather, it's about picking items that are rich in good fats and low in carbohydrates carefully. If you aren't sure where to start, don't be scared. Some very healthy, excellent keto meals are out there appealing to be consumed.

### 2.1 Keto Breakfast Recipes

## 1. HIGH PROTEIN COTTAGE CHEESE OMELET

## Serving: 1

**Preparation time: 5 minutes**

**Nutritional Values: 250kcal Calories | 18g Fat | 4 g Carbs | 18.7g Proteins**

## Ingredients

- 2 eggs - large
- 1 tbsp. of whole milk or 2% milk
- Kosher salt about 1/8 tsp.
- Pinch of black pepper, freshly ground,
- 1/2 tbsp. of butter - unsalted
- 1 cup spinach (about 1 ounce)
- Cottage cheese 3 tbsp.

## Directions

1. In a moderate pan, put the eggs, milk, salt, & pepper and stir until the whites & yolks are thoroughly combined, and the eggs are a little viscous.

2. In an 8-inch non - stick roasting pan over medium heat, add the butter. Flip the pan until the butter covers the bottom equally. Include the spinach and simmer for around 30 seconds before it is ripened. Put the eggs in and turn the pan directly so that the eggs cover the whole bottom.

3. To softly pull and move the cooked eggs from the sides into the middle of the pan, use either a silicone or rubber spatula, leaving room for the raw eggs and creating waves in the omelet. Rig a spatula underneath the edges to enable raw eggs to run beneath the cooked part, holding and swiveling the pan. Cook for around 2 minutes until the sides are settled, and the middle is moist but no longer soft or gooey.

4. Let the pan away from the heat. Whisk over half the eggs with the cottage cheese. Cover the egg carefully over the filling using a spatula. On a plate, transfer the omelet.

## 2. DEVILED EGGS

**Serving: 4-6**

**Preparation time: 15-20 minutes**

**Nutritional values: 280kcal Calories | 23g Fat | 3.4g Carbs | 15g Proteins**

**Ingredients**

- 12 eggs - large
- 8 oz. of full-fat cream cheese, warmed for 1 hour or more at room temperature,
- Kosher salt about 1/2 teaspoon
- 1 shred of black pepper
- 2 tablespoons of all the bagel seasoning

## Directions

1. A dozen eggs become hardboiled according to your chosen method. (The most critical part is to layer with ice water, raise to a boil, then lift from the heat and leave for 8 to 10 minutes to remain.) In an ice bucket, soak and chill the eggs. And peel them.

2. Cut the eggs laterally in half and use a tiny spoon to pick the yolks out and put them in a dish.

3. Take the cream cheese and transfer it to the yolks into rough parts. Use a hand beater or stick mixer to mix until smooth and blended, starting at lower speeds and then at high speed. Bang in the pepper and salt. Uh, taste. If needed, tweak the seasonings.

4. Load the egg whites with the yolk mixture using a spoon or piping bag. (It would be stiff; to soften it any further if possible, microwave it in very fast bursts of 2 to 3 seconds.)

5. With the all-bagel seasoning, dust the tops of the loaded eggs appropriately. In two hours, serve.

# 3. 90 SECOND KETO BREAD

**Serving: 1**

**Preparation time: 90 seconds**

**Nutritional values: 99kcal Calories | 8.5g Fat | 2g Carbs | 3.9g Proteins**

**Instructions**

- 1 egg - large
- 1 spoonful of milk
- Olive oil about 1 tablespoon
- 1 tablespoon flour of coconut
- 1 tablespoon flour of almonds or hazelnuts
- 1/4 tsp. powder for baking
- Pinch of salt

**Add-ins optional:**

- 1/4 cup of grated cheese

- 1 tbsp. scallions or herbs chopped

## Directions

1. In a small cup, mix together the egg, milk, oil, coconut flour, almond flour, baking powder, and salt. If using, incorporate cheese and scallions or herbs and mix to blend.

2. To induce any air bubbles to lift and burst, pour into a wide microwave-safe mug and strike the bottom tightly on the counter multiple times. Reheat for 1 minute, 30 seconds, on maximum.

3. On a chopping board, transpose the mug and enable the bread to drop out. Slice into 1/2-inch-thick strips crosswise. For the toast, heat a teaspoon of oil across moderate flame in a small pan until it glistens. Add the strips and toast, around 30 seconds on either side, before golden-brown.

# 4. KETO FRITTATA

**Serving: 4-6**

**Preparation time: 25 minutes**

**Nutritional values: 155kcal Calories | 8.9g Fat | 11.4g Carbs | 7.9g Proteins**

**Instructions**

- 6 large eggs, sufficient for the ingredients to fill
- Heavy cream 1/4 cup
- 1 tsp. of kosher salt, split-up
- 4 thick-cut bacon (8 oz.) pieces, diced (optional)
- 2 tiny, stripped, and finely diced Yukon gold potatoes
- 1/4 tsp. of black pepper, freshly ground

- 2 cups of spinach (2 ounces)
- Garlic 2 cloves, chopped.
- 2 tsp. of fresh leaves of thyme
- 1 cup of Gruyere, Fontina, or Cheddar crushed cheese

## Directions

1. Preheat oven. In the center of the oven, position a brace and warm it to 400 °F.

2. Stir together the cream and eggs. In a medium bowl, stir together the eggs, whipping cream, and 1/2 teaspoon salt; hold.

3. Just prepare the bacon. Put the bacon in a non - stick 10-12-inch cold cooking pan or cast-iron skillet, and keep the heat to moderate. Cook the bacon until translucent, stirring regularly, for 8 to 10 minutes. Move the bacon to a paper towel-lined dish with a slotted spoon and skim off all but 2 tbsp. of the fat. (If the bacon is excluded, heat the pan with 2 tablespoons of oil, then finish incorporating the potatoes).

4. Simmer the potatoes in the fat of the bacon. Mix the potatoes and spray with the pepper and the remaining 1/2 teaspoon salt. Switch the pan to a moderate flame. Heat, stirring regularly, for 4 to 6 minutes, until soft and golden brown.

5. Crumble the spinach with thyme & garlic. Put the spinach, garlic, and thyme in the pan and cook, mixing, for 30 seconds to 1 minute, or until the spinach is wilted. Transfer the bacon again to the skillet and swirl to spread uniformly.

6. Add some cheese. Scattered the vegetables, compressed with a spatula, into an even layer. Over the top, spread the cheese and let it only begin to melt.

7. In the pan, add the egg mixture. Place over the vegetables and cheese with the egg mixture. To be sure that the eggs settle equally over all the vegetables, rotate the skillet. Wait for a minute or two before you observe the eggs starting to set at the ends of the pan.

8. Around 8 to 10 minutes, oven the frittata. Bake for 8 to 10 minutes unless the eggs are ready. Cut a tiny slit in the middle of the frittata to test. Bake for a few more minutes if uncooked eggs run into the cut; if the eggs are fixed, take the frittata out of the oven. At the end of cooking, hold the frittata underneath the broiler for a couple of minutes for a crisped, charred layer.

9. For 5 minutes, chill in the skillet, then cut into slices and serve.

## 5. CHEESE, HAM, AND EGG WRAPS

**Serving: 4**

**Preparation time: 15-20 minutes**

**Nutritional values: 371kcal calories | 27g Fat | %g Carbs | 27g Proteins**

## Ingredients

- 8 eggs - large
- 4 tsp. of Water
- 2 tsp. of all-purpose or cornstarch flour
- Half a teaspoon of fine salt
- 4 tsp. of coconut or vegetable oil
- 1 1/3 cups of Swiss grated cheese
- 4 ounces of ham extremely thinly sliced
- 1 1/3 cups of watercress loosely wrapped

## Directions

1. In a wide bowl, put the eggs, water, flour or cornflour, and salt, and stir until the starch or cornflour is fully dissolved.

2. In a 12-inch non - stick saucepan, heat 1 tsp. Of oil unless glinting, over moderate flame. To cover the surface with the oil, move the pan. To brush the bottom part in a thin coating, incorporate 1/2 cup of the egg mixture and stir. Cook for 3 to 6 minutes before the wrapping is fully set on the sides and on the surface (the top may be a little damp but should be apparently set).

3. Soften the sides of the wrap using a wide spatula and move it under the wrap, ensuring that it will slide across the pan quickly. With the spatula, turn the wrap. Slather 1/3 cup of cheese instantly over the wrap and simmer for around 1 minute before the second side is ready. Drop it onto a chopping board or work surface (the cheese may not be completely melted yet). Put a single coat of ham over the egg when it is still hot. Put 1/3 of a cup of watercress in the middle of the wrap. Firmly roll it up.

4. Repeat the leftover wraps by cooking and filling them. Slice each wrap crosswise into 6 (1-inch) bits using a steak knife.

# 6. BACON GRUYERE EGG BITES

**Serving: 9**

**Preparation time: 10-20 minutes**

**Nutritional values: 208kcal Calories | 18g Fat | 1g Carbs | 11g Proteins**

**Ingredients**

- Fat or butter of bacon, to coat the pan
- 9 large eggs
- 3/4 cup Gruyere cheese grated (2 1/4 oz.)

- 1/3 cup (about 2 1/2 oz.) cream cheese
- Kosher salt about 1/2 teaspoon
- 6 pieces of thick-cut, cooked, and imploded bacon

## Directions

1. In the center of the oven, place a rack and warm it to 350°F. Graciously cover an 8x8-inch (broiler-safe if you like a crisped top) cooking dish with bacon fat or butter.

2. Put the eggs, Gruyere, cream cheese, and salt in a mixer and combine for around 1 minute, at moderate speed, until quite smooth. Drop it into the pan for baking. Slather bacon with it. With aluminum foil, cover firmly.

3. Take the oven rack out from the oven midway. Upon on the oven rack, put a roasting tray. Put in 6 extremely hot tap water pots. Place the baking dish in the hot skillet with the eggs. Bake until the center is just ready, 55 minutes to 1 hour.

4. Pull the roasting pan from the oven cautiously. Remove the roasting pan from the baking dish and unfold it. (For a browned surface: Heat the oven to sauté. Sauté 4 to 5 minutes before the top is golden-brown.) Slice and serve into 9 squares.

# 7. RADISH TURNIP AND FRIED EGGS HASH WITH GREEN GARLIC

Serving: 2

**Preparation time: 10-12 minutes**

**Nutritional values: 392kcal calories | 34g Fat | 10g Carbs | 13g Proteins**

**Ingredients**

- 2 to 3 tiny turnips (approximately 1 1/2 cups cubed) clipped, peeled, and sliced into 3/4-inch cubes
- 4 to 5 tiny, rinsed and clipped radishes, and sliced into 3/4-inch cubes (approximately 1 1/2 cubed cups)
- Crushed Salt of the Sea
- Pepper freshly crushed
- 2 tbsp. of grapeseed oil, or other heat-tolerant, neutral oil
- 1 green garlic stalk, clipped and diced (just white and light green parts)
- 2 spoonful's of unsalted butter

- Four eggs
- 1 tablespoon parsley chopped

**Directions**

1. Place the water in a wide skillet and raise it to a boil. Stir in 2 teaspoons of sea salt. Transfer to a bowl with a slotted spoon, skim off any extra water and set it aside. Simmer turnip cubes only until moist, 3 to 4 minutes. Next, quickly boil the radishes for 30 to 60 seconds; scrape with a slotted spoon in a pan, skim off any extra water, and set it aside.

2. Place a sauté pan of cast iron over moderate flame. Include the grapeseed oil and add the turnips & radishes when warm, and pinch the sea salt and pepper with each one. Cook for 8 minutes or until golden-brown, flipping vegetables just once or twice. Switch the heat to medium, bring in the green garlic and simmer for a minute or so. Place the vegetables to the edges, melt the butter in the center of the pan, and add the eggs. Cook unearthed for 4 to 6 minutes for over-easy eggs; close pan for 3 minutes for over-medium eggs, then unfold and continue to cook only until whites are ready, 2 to 3 minutes further. To taste, finish with chopped parsley and sea salt and pepper. Instantly serve.

## 8. CAULIFLOWER RICE BURRITO BOWLS

**Serving: 4**

**Preparation time: 20-25 minutes**

**Nutritional values: 374kcal Calories | 15g Fat | 46g Carbs | 21g Protein**

**Ingredients**

- 1 (15-ounce) canned washed and cleaned black beans.
- 1 cup of corn kernels - frozen
- 2 spoonful's of water
- Chili powder about 1/2 teaspoon
- 1/2 teaspoon of cumin powder
- 3/4 teaspoon of kosher salt, distributed
- 1 tablespoon of olive oil
- One cauliflower of a medium head (just around 1 1/2 lbs.), riced (or one 16oz sack riced cauliflower)
- 1/3 cup of fresh cilantro minced, distributed

- 1/4 cup of lime juice, freshly extracted (from 2 to 3 lemons)
- 1 cup roasted chicken chopped or shredded (optional), warmed if necessary
- 1 cup of gallo pico de or salsa
- One large, drained, pitted, and diced avocado

**Directions**

1. In a small pan, put the beans, corn, water, chili powder, cumin, and 1/4 tsp. over moderate flame. Cook for 3 to 5 minutes, mixing periodically until hot. Distance yourself from the steam.

2. In the meantime, over a moderate flame, heat the oil in a wide, large skillet until it shimmers. Transfer the cauliflower and the residual 1/2 teaspoon salt to the mixture. Process until the cauliflower is cooked through though soft, 3 to 5 minutes, mixing periodically. Remove from the heat. Transfer the cilantro and lime juice to 1/4 cup and mix to blend.

3. Divide into four bowls the riced cauliflower. Cover with the mixture of bean and corn, chicken if used, pico de gallo or salsa, and pieces of avocado. Slather with the cilantro that persists and serve hot.

# 9. KETO LOAF

**Serving: 1**

**Preparation time: 10-12 minutes**

**Nutritional values: 239kcal Calories | 22g Fat | 4g carbs | 8g Proteins**

**Ingredients**

- Two cups of fine powdered almond flour, especially brands like King Arthur
- 1 tsp. powder for baking
- 1/2 tsp. of gum xanthan
- Kosher salt about 1\2 tsp.
- 7 eggs - large

- 8 tbsp. (1 stick) of melted and chilled unsalted butter
- 2 tbsp. of concentrated, processed, and chilled coconut oil

**Directions**

1. In the center of the oven, place a rack and warm it to 351°F. Cover the bottom part of a parchment paper 9x5-inch metallic loaf pan, having the surplus spill around the long sides to create a loop. Just set aside.

2. In a wide dish, mix together the flour of almond, powder for baking, xanthan gum, as well as salt. Just placed back.

3. Put the eggs in a bowl equipped with the whisk extension of a stand blender. Beat at moderate pressure until soft and drippy. Lower the level to moderate, incorporate the butter and oil of coconut gradually, and whisk unless well mixed. Lessen the intensity to medium, incorporate the mixture of almond flour gradually, and mix unless mixed. Rise the pace to moderate and beat for around 1 minute before the mixture thickens.

4. Pour and scrape the top into the primed pan. Bake for 45 to 55 minutes unless a knife placed in the middle comes out clean. Let it cool for around ten minutes in the pan. Take the loaf over the skillet, grab the parchment paper, and shift it to a cutting board. Cool it down completely until slicing.

# 10. BREAKFAST SALAD

**Serving: 4**

**Preparation time: 10 minutes**

**Nutritional values: 425kcal Calories | 34g Fat | 16g Carbs | 17g Proteins**

**Ingredients**

- Spinach 8 Oz (about 6 packed cups)
- 1/2 a cup of blueberries
- 1 medium-sized avocado, chopped
- 1/3 cup red roasted quinoa
- 1/4 cup of pumpkin seeds - toasted

- Bacon - 6 strips
- 4 eggs of large size
- 1/4 cup of apple cider vinegar
- 2 tsp. of honey
- Kosher salt about 1\2 tsp.

## Directions

1. In a large bowl, add the spinach, avocado, berries, pumpkin seeds, and quinoa and toss them to mix. Distribute the salad into deep plates or pots.

2. Put the bacon over moderate heat in a large cast-iron pan. Cook until the fat has dried out and the bacon is crunchy, tossing halfway around for a total of around 10 minutes. Shift the bacon to a tray that is lined with paper towels. Cut the bacon into little crumbles until it is cold.

3. Lower the heat and fry the eggs to the perfect braising in the dried bacon fat. Keep the pan away from the heat. Place the toppled bacon and an egg on top of each salad.

4. Upon emulsification, mix the vinegar, honey, and salt into the residual bacon fat in the dish. Sprinkle over the salad with the warm dressing and serve promptly.

## 2.2 Keto Lunch & Dinner Recipes

## 1. CAULIFLOWER FRIED RICE

**Serving: 4**

**Preparation time: 20- 25 minutes**

**Nutritional values: 108kcal Calories | 1g Fat | 21g Carbs | 7g Proteins**

**Ingredients**

**For Fried Rice**

- 1 cauliflower head, sliced into cloves
- Balanced Oil 2 tbsp. (such as vegetable, coconut, or peanut)

- 1 bunch of finely sliced scallions
- 3 cloves of garlic, chopped
- 1 tbsp. natural ginger diced
- 2 peeled and finely chopped carrots
- 2 stalks of celery, chopped
- 1 bell pepper, red, chopped
- 1 cup of peas - frozen
- 2 tbsp. vinegar for rice
- 3 spoonful's of soy sauce
- Sriracha 2 tsp., or enough to taste

## For Garnishing

- Balanced oil about 1tbsp. (such as vegetable, coconut, or peanut)
- Four eggs
- Salt and black pepper finely processed
- 4 tbsp. of fresh cilantro, diced
- 4 tbsp. of scallions thinly diced
- 4 tsp. of seeds of sesame

## Directions

1. **For Fried Rice:** Pump the cauliflower in the mixing bowl for 2 or 3 minutes before the mishmash resembles rice. Just set aside.

2. Heat oil over a moderate flame in a wide skillet. Include the scallions, garlic, and ginger and mix for around 1 minute, unless aromatic.

3. Incorporate the carrots, celery & red bell pepper, and braise for 9 to 11 minutes until the veggies are soft.

4. Add the cauliflower rice, then stir-fry for another 3 to 5 minutes, once it starts to turn golden. To blend, mix in the frozen peas and toss properly.

5. To combine, incorporate rice vinegar, Sriracha, and soy sauce & swirl. Just set aside.

6. **For Garnishing:** Add the oil in a large skillet over moderate to high flame. Crack the eggs straight into the skillet and stir for 3 to 4 minutes before the whites are assertive, but the yolks are still watery. With pepper and salt, sprinkle each one.

7. Distribute the cauliflower rice into four dishes to serving and serve each one with a fried egg. Sprinkle with 1 tablespoon of cilantro, 1 tablespoon of scallions, and 1 teaspoon of sesame seeds on each dish. Instantly serve then.

## 2. LOW CARB THAI CURRY SOUP

**Serving: 6**

**Preparation time: 22 minutes**

**Nutritional values: 324kcal Calories | 27g Fat | 7g Carbs | 15g Proteins**

## Ingredients

- 4 Leg pieces of boneless skinless chicken,
- 14.5 ounces (411.07 g) full-fat coconut milk
- 2 tsp. of Thai paste of yellow curry
- 2 tsp. of fish sauce
- Three tsp. of Soy Sauce
- 1 tsp. of Agave or honey nectar
- 2 green Scallions minced
- Garlic 4 cloves, minced
- 2 inch (2 inches) coarsely chopped diced ginger

## Veggies to add in soup

- One Can of Straw Mushrooms (optional)
- 74.5 g (1/2 cup) of Cherry Tomatoes, half-sliced
- Cilantro, 1/4 cup (4 g), diced
- 3 green Scallions diced
- 1 lime, juiced

## Directions

## For the Instant Pot

1. Put the essential soup components and lock in an Instant Pot.
2. Process it under heat for 12 minutes by using the SOUP key. The soup button avoids it from boiling and extracting the coconut milk.
3. Discharge the pressure immediately and detach and cut the chicken. Place it in the broth again.

4. Transfer the warm broth to the vegetables. In the hot broth, you want to bring them a little scorching but not to mold them though you can actually taste the flavor of the vegetables and herbs.

## For the Slow Cooker

1. In a slow cooker, put the essential soup ingredients and steam for 8 hours on lower or 4 hours on average.

2. Over the last half-hour, place in vegetables and herbs. In the hot broth, you want to bring them a little scorching but not to mold them though you can actually taste the flavor of the vegetables and herbs.

3. Remove the chicken and cut it. Place it in the broth again.

- It's actually cheaper to purchase Thai Yellow Curry Paste than to prepare it. At your nearest Asian food store, you will find it.

- With the provided directions, prepare this in your Instant Pot or slow cooker. If required, you may use heavy whipping cream for coconut milk.

# 3. JALAPENO POPPER SOUP

**Serving: 3**

**Preparation time: 25 minutes**

**Nutritional values: 446kcal Calories | 35g Fat | 4g Carbs | 28g Proteins**

**Ingredients**

- 4 bacon strips
- 2 spoonful's of butter
- Medium-sized 1/2 onion, chopped
- 1/4 cup of pickled, diced jalapenos
- 2 cups broth of chicken
- 2 cups of shredded chicken, cooked
- Cream cheese 4 ounces
- Heavy cream 1/3 cup

- 1 cup of Fresh Cheddar Shredded
- 1/4 tsp. powdered garlic
- Pepper and salt, to taste
- If needed, 1/2 tsp. xanthan gum for thick soup [Optional]

## Directions

1. Fry the bacon in a pan. Crumble when cooked and put aside. Place a large pot over the moderate flame while the bacon cooks. Include the onion and butter and simmer until the onion becomes porous.

2. Transfer the jalapenos and half the crumbled bacon to the pot.

3. Pour in the broth of the chicken and the shredded chicken. Take to a boil, then cook for 20 minutes, and reduce.

4. Put the cream cheese in a medium bowl and microwave for around 20 seconds; once soft until smooth, mix. Stir the cream cheese and the heavy cream into the soup. It may take a few minutes for the cream cheese to be completely integrated. Turn the heat off.

5. Include the shredded cheese, and whisk until it is completely melted. Add xanthan gum at this stage if the thick soup is preferred.

6. Serve with the leftover bacon on top.

# 4. PEPPERS & SAUSAGES

**Serving: 6**

**Preparation time: 2 hrs.5 minutes**

**Nutritional values: 313kcal Calories | 22g Fat | 11g Carbs | 16g Proteins**

**Ingredients**

- 1 tablespoon olive oil
- Six medium links of Pork sausage
- 3 of the large Bell peppers (cut into strips)
- 1 onion of large size (cut into half, the same size as the pepper shreds)
- Garlic 6 Cloves (minced)
- 1 tbsp. seasoning Italian
- Sea salt about 1/2 tsp.
- Black pepper 1/4 teaspoon

- 1 and a half cups of Marinara sauce

**Directions**

1. To activate a kitchen timer whilst you cook, toggle on the times in the directions below.

2. Heat the oil over moderate heat in a large pan. Include the sausage links until its warm. Cook on either side for around 2 minutes, only until golden brown on the outer side. (Inside, they will not be prepared.)

3. In the meantime, in a slow cooker, add the bell peppers, onions, garlic, Italian spices, salt, & pepper. Toss it to coat it. Softly spill the marinara sauce over the veggies.

4. Once the sausage links are golden brown, put them on top of the veggies in the slow cooker.

5. Cook on low flame or 2-3 hours on high flame for 4-5 hours, unless the sausages are cooked completely.

# 5. SHRIMPS WITH CAULIFLOWER GRITS AND ARUGULA

**Serving: 4**

**Preparation time: 25-30 minutes**

**Nutritional values: 123kcal Calories | 5g Fat | 3g Carbs | 16g proteins**

**Ingredients**

**For Spicy Shrimp**

- 1 pound of cleaned and roasted shrimp
- 1 tablespoon of paprika
- 2 teaspoons of powdered garlic
- 1/2 tsp. of pepper cayenne

- 1 tablespoon of olive oil extra virgin

- Salt and black pepper freshly processed

- GRITS of CAULIFLOWER

- Unsalted butter about 1 tablespoon

- Riced cauliflower about four cups

- 1cup of milk

- 1/2 cup of goat's crushed cheese

- Salt & black pepper freshly processed

## For Garlic Arugula

- 1 tablespoon of olive oil extra virgin

- 3 cloves of garlic, finely minced

- 4 cups of baby arugula

- Salt & black pepper freshly processed

## Directions

1. **Prepare the Spicy Shrimp:** Put the shrimp in a big plastic zip-top pack. Mix the paprika in a tiny bowl with the garlic powder as well as the cayenne to blend. Place the mixture with the shrimp into the packet and shake well before the spices have covered them. Refrigerate the grits while preparing them.

2. **Prepare the Cauliflower "Grits":** Melt the butter over a moderate flame in a wide bowl. Integrate the cauliflower rice and simmer for 2 to 3 minutes once it sheds some of its steam.

3. Whisk in half the milk and raise it to a boil. Continue to boil, stirring regularly, for 6 to 8 minutes, before some milk is consumed by the cauliflower.

4. Add the leftover milk and boil for another 10 minutes before the mixture is smooth and fluffy. Mix in the cheese from the goat and add salt and pepper. Just hold warm.

5. **Prepare Garlic Arugula:** Warm olive oil over moderate heat in a large pan. Add the garlic and simmer for 1 minute unless tangy. Include the arugula and simmer for 3 to 4 minutes, unless softened. Use salt and pepper to season, take from the pan, and put aside.

6. Heat the olive oil over low heat in the same pan. Include shrimp and simmer for 4 to 5 minutes until completely cooked. Use salt and pepper to season.

7. Divide the grits into four dishes to serve, then top each one with a fourth of the arugula & a quarter of the shrimp. Immediately serve.

# 6. CHICKEN CHILI WHITE

**Serving: 4**

**Preparation time: 35-45 minutes**

**Nutritional values: 481kcal Calories | 30g Fat | 5g Carbs | 39g Proteins**

**Ingredients**

- 1 lb. breast of chicken
- Chicken broth about 1.5 cups

- 2 cloves of garlic, thinly chopped
- 1 can of sliced green chills
- 1 jalapeno sliced
- 1 green pepper chopped
- 1/4 cup onion finely chopped
- Four tablespoons of butter
- 1/4 cup of heavy whipped cream
- Four-ounce cream cheese
- 2 teaspoons of cumin
- 1 teaspoon of oregano
- Cayenne 1/4 teaspoon (additional)
- To taste: salt & black pepper

## Directions

1. Season the chicken with cumin, cayenne, oregano, salt, and black pepper in a wide pan.
2. Braise both sides unless golden, under medium-high heat,
3. Transfer the broth to the pan, cover, and cook for 15-20 minutes or until the chicken is completely cooked.
4. Melt the butter in a moderate pan while the chicken is frying.
5. In the pan, incorporate the chills, chopped jalapeno, green pepper, and onion, and simmer until the vegetables soften.
6. Add the chopped garlic and simmer for an extra 30 seconds, switching off the heat and put aside.
7. When the chicken is fully done, slice it with a fork and transfer it to the broth.
8. In a chicken & broth pan, incorporate the sautéed veggies and cook for 10 minutes.

9. Soften the cream cheese in the microwave in a mixing bowl so you can blend it (~20 sec)

10. Mix the cream cheese and heavy whipped cream

11. Add the mixture of chicken and vegetables into the pot and whisk rapidly.

12. Simmer for an extra 15 minutes.

13. Serve with preferred toppings such as cheese from the pepper jack, slices of avocado, coriander, sour cream.

## 7. BOWL OF CHICKEN ENCHILADA

**Serving: 4**

**Preparation time: 40-50 minutes**

**Nutritional values: 570kcal Calories | 40g Fat | 6g Carbs | 38g Proteins**

## Ingredients

- 2 spoonful's of coconut oil (for searing chicken)
- 1 pound of chicken thighs that are boneless, skinless
- 3/4 cup sauce of red enchilada
- 1/4 of a cup of water
- 1/4 cup onion, minced
- 1-4 oz. green chills Can - sliced

## Toppings

- 1 Avocado, sliced
- 1 cup of cheese, crushed
- 1/4 cup of pickled jalapenos, diced
- 1/2 of a cup of sour cream
- 1 tomato Roma, diced

## Directions

1. Heat up the coconut oil on a moderate flame in a pan or a Dutch oven. Braise the chicken thighs unless finely brown when hot.

2. Place in the enchilada sauce as well as the water. After this, add the onion and also the green chilies. Lower the heat to a boil and cover it. Cook the chicken for 17-25 minutes or until the chicken is juicy and heated to an inner temperature of approximately 165 degrees.

3. Remove the chicken cautiously and put it on a chopping board. Then put it back into the pot. Cut or shred chicken (your preference). To retain flavor, let the chicken boil uncovered for an extra 10 minutes and enable the sauce to minimize some more.

4. For serving, cover with avocado, cheese, jalapeno, tomato, sour cream, or any other toppings you want. Feel free to adjust them to your taste.

If preferred, serve individually or over cauliflower rice; just refresh your personal nutrition details as required.

## 8. CHIPOTLE HEALTHY KETO PULLED PORK

**Serving: 10**

**Preparation time: 8 hrs.15 minutes**

**Nutritional values: 430kcal Calories | 34g Fat | 3g Carbs | 27g Proteins**

**Ingredients**

- 1 Mid-yellow onion chopped

- 1 cup of water
- 2 tablespoons of fresh garlic diced
- 1 tablespoon of Coconut Sugar
- 1 tablespoon of salt
- 1 teaspoon of chili powder
- 1/2 teaspoon of cumin powder
- 1/2 Tablespoon Adobo sauce
- Smoked paprika 1/4 teaspoons
- 3 1/2-4 lbs. pork shoulder, Extra fat should be removed
- Whole wheat or hamburger buns without gluten OR salad wraps for serving
- Paleo ranch, to be garnished
- Coleslaw blend for optional garnish
- Lime Juice, to be garnished
- Green Tabasco for garnishing

## Directions

1. Cut the onion and chop the garlic, and put it in the base of the slow cooker—a spill in a cup of water.

2. In a small bowl, mix all the ingredients for the seasoning and set it aside.

3. Slice off the pork shoulder some large, noticeable parts of fat and spread it all over with the seasoning until it is uniformly covered.

4. Over the top of the garlic, onions & water, add the pork and simmer until soft and juicy, 6-8 hours on maximum or 8-10 hours on reduced.

5. If the pork is cooked, extract much of the liquid from the crockpot and put the solids directly into the crockpot (which comprises the garlic and onions).

6. On a chopping board, move the pork and slice it with two forks.

7. In the slow cooker, shift the sliced pork back and combine with the onions and garlic. Cover unless ready to be served, and keep it warm.

8. On a bun or lettuce, place the pulled pork, served with a ranch coleslaw blend and a pinch of lime juice as well as green tabasco.

9. Enjoy.

## 9. STIR FRY ZOODLE

**Serving: 4**

**Preparation time: 15-22 minutes**

**Nutritional values: 113kcal Calories | 3g Fat | 20g Carbs | 6g Proteins**

**Ingredients**

- Sesame oil 11/2 tsp. (or 1 tbsp. of olive oil)
- 1 bunch of thinly chopped scallions
- 2 cloves of garlic, chopped
- 1 tablespoon of fresh ginger, diced

- Two carrots, chopped into thin strands
- One red pepper bell, cut into small strands,
- Two cups of snap peas
- Four zucchini, sliced into noodles (using a utensil like this)
- 1/4 cup of soy sauce
- 3 tbsp. vinegar for rice
- 1/4 cup of fresh cilantro, diced

## Directions

1. Add the oil in a wide sauté pan over medium heat. Integrate the scallions, garlic, and ginger and simmer for 1 to 2 minutes, unless aromatic.

2. Include the bell pepper, carrots, snap peas & zucchini noodles. Sauté for 5 to 6 minutes until the vegetables just start to become soft.

3. Integrate the soy sauce & rice vinegar and proceed to cook unless the vegetables are quite soft and juicy, frequently tossing, for another 3 to 4 minutes.

4. Seasoned with cilantro, serve hot.

# 10. TEX MEX CHICKEN SALAD

**Serving: 4**

**Preparation time: 25 minutes**

**Nutritional values: 546kcal Calories | 41g Fat | 12g Carbs | 30g Proteins**

**Ingredients**

- For the seasoning of the fajita:
- 2 tsp. of powdered chili
- 1 tsp. of cumin
- 1 tsp. of powdered garlic
- 1 teaspoon powdered onion
- 1 tsp. of paprika. smoked
- 1/2 tsp. of or to taste salt

**For the fajitas**

- Two spoonful's of olive oil
- 1/2 tsp. ground mustard OR 1 tbsp. of Dijon mustard as required
- 1 lemon juice
- 2 medium breasts of chicken hammered to even density
- 2 tablespoons divided butter
- 4 finely diced medium bell peppers into slices
- 1 medium red onion finely sliced into slices
- 2-3 leaves of buttered lettuce
- 2-3 leaves of romaine lettuce

## To serve

- Slices of lime
- Avocado sliced

## Directions

1. Mix all the ingredients for the condiments in a tiny compostable jar. Enclose well and squish. For bell peppers, save 1 1/2 tsp.

2. Integrate two tbsp. of olive oil, lemon juice, and 5 tsp. of fajita condiments in a wide, zip lock bag. In the bag, add the chicken and secure it. Push the marinade into the chicken and enable the vegetables to marinate while preparing them (or freeze in the fridge unless ready to use).

3. Cut the bell peppers as well as onions.

4. Heat 1 tbsp. of butter over moderate heat in a large skillet. Add the onions and cook for approximately 4-5 minutes, or until tender and succulent. Transfer the bell peppers and squirt 1 1/2 tsp. of fajita condiments with the restrained ones. Cook for almost 3-5 minutes if you like the peppers with a lovely crunch. And if you like it softer, end up leaving it on for about two to three minutes long. Set aside and move to a plate.

5. Melt 1 residual tablespoon of butter and brown the chicken in the same pan. Cook for 5-6 minutes, or until properly cooked.

6. In a wide salad bowl or tray, organize the lettuce and top it with chicken as well as bell peppers. Add your chosen sliced avocados, lime slices, and any other seasonings.

## 11. KETO BROCCOLI CHEDDAR SOUP

**Serving: 4**

**Preparation time: 20 minutes**

**Nutritional values: 285kcal Calories | 25g Fat | 3g Carbs | 12g Proteins**

## Ingredients

- 2 spoonful's of butter
- 1/8 cup of onion, white
- 1/2 tsp. of finely chopped garlic
- 2 cups of broth of chicken
- Pepper and salt, to taste
- 1 cup of broccoli, cut into bite-sized pieces
- 1 spoon of cream cheese
- Heavy whipping cream 1/4 cup
- 1 cup of cheddar cheese, crushed
- Bacon 2 loaves, cooked and Imploded (Optional)
- 1/2 tsp. of gum xanthan (Optional)

## Directions

1. Simmer the onion and garlic with butter in a wide pot over medium heat until the onions are seamless and textured.
2. Add broth as well as broccoli to the pot. Until soft, cook broccoli. Add the salt, pepper, and seasoning you want.
3. Put the cream cheese in a medium bowl and heat for ~30 seconds in the microwave until smooth and easy to mix.
4. Mix in the soup with heavy whipping cream and cream cheese; bring to the boil.
5. Turn off the heat and mix the cheddar cheese swiftly.
6. If required, stir in the xanthan gum. Allow for stiffening.
7. Serve hot with implodes of bacon (if desired)

# 12. SPICY THAI BUTTERNUT SQUASH SOUP

**Serving: 4**

**Preparation time: 30 minutes**

**Nutritional values: 450kcal Calories | 35g Fat | 35g Carbs | 8g proteins**

**Ingredients**

- 11/2 tbsp. coconut oil, refined
- 1 large onion, yellow, sliced
- 1/4 cup of a paste of red curry
- One 2-inch slice of grated or finely chopped garlic
- Four teaspoons of cloves of garlic, diced

- 4 cups vegetable stock with low sodium or water
- 1 peeled and finely diced medium butternut squash (about 41/2 cups)
- One 13.5-ounce coconut milk full-fat can
- 1/4 cup cashew butter or almond butter in natural form
- Lower tamari 1 tbsp.
- 1 tablespoon maple syrup or nectar of Agave
- Kosher salt about 1 tsp., plus more to flavor
- Three teaspoons of freshly pressed lemon juice
- 1/2 cup of fresh, chopped cilantro, plus more for garnishing
- Serve with coconut yogurt, roasted peanuts, scallions & sesame seeds

## Directions

1. Choose the Instant Pot Sauté mode, then add the coconut oil after several minutes. When the oil is warm, add a bit of salt to the onion, and then cook for 6 to 7 minutes before it starts to brown. Transfer the curry paste, ginger, and garlic; simmer for about 1 minute, constantly stirring, until quite tangy.

2. Spill the stock in and use a wooden spoon on the bottom of the pot to pick off some browned pieces. Stir in butternut squash, coconut milk, tamari, salt, cashew butter, and maple syrup. To blend properly, mix.

3. Shield the cover and seal the pressure release. Choose the high-pressure setting for the soup and specify the cooking time to 12 minutes.

4. Enable an organic pressure release for 5 minutes when the timer goes off, and then undergo a speedy pressure release.

5. Open the pot, add the lime juice and mix. Mix, so you have a nice and creamy broth using an electric mixer. Conversely, using a dish towel to shield the mixer cap to keep steam from spreading, you should pass the broth in batches to a mixer.

6. Stir in the minced cilantro until the broth is pureed — seasoning with coconut yogurt, peanuts, sesame seeds, and scallions as needed.

## 13. KETO PHO RECIPE

**Serving: 4**

**Preparation time: 35 minutes**

**Nutritional values: 220kcal Calories | 5g Fat | 8g Carbs | 33g Proteins**

**Ingredients**

- 4 Entire Star Anise
- 2 entire pods of Cardamom
- 2 entire sticks of Cinnamon
- 2 Whole Cloves
- 1 tbsp. seeds of Coriander
- 1 tsp. of ginger
- 8 cups of bone broth of beef

- 1 tablespoon of Fish sauce
- 1 tbsp. Allulose Mix of Besti Monk Fruit (optional, to taste)
- Salt (optional, to taste)

**Soup Pho**:

- Flank steak 12 oz. (trimmed, or sirloin)
- 2 large Zucchinis (spiraled into zoodles)

**Pho toppings optional:**

- Thai basil
- Cilantro
- Wedges of lime
- Slices of red chili pepper (or jalapeno peppers)
- Scallions
- Sriracha

**Directions**

1. For 30 minutes, put the steak in the refrigerator to make it easy to slice finely.

2. In the meantime, over moderate heat, warm a Dutch oven, minus oil. Bring the star anise, pods of cardamom, sticks of cinnamon, garlic, seeds of coriander, and fresh ginger. Toast, until aromatic, for 2-3 minutes.

3. Combine the fish sauce as well as bone broth. Mix together — Cook the pho broth and stew for 30 minutes.

4. In the meantime, to make zoodles out from the zucchini, use a spiralizer. Split the noodles from the zucchini into 4 bowls.

5. Pull it out and slice rather thinly against the grain until the steak in the refrigerator is stable. Put the steak inside each bowl on top of the zoodles.

6. Mix in the sweetener to disintegrate (if used) and modify the salt to taste whenever the broth is finished simmering. In a different pot or bowl, extract the soup. Discard all the spices that are trapped in the strainer.

7. Although the broth is already simmering, spill it over the preparing bowls instantly, making sure that the steak is immersed, so it cooks completely. (Conversely, the steak should first be stirred into the boiling broth.)

8. Thai basil, coriander, lemon slices, jalapeno or chili pepper strips, scallions, and Sriracha, and garnish with condiments of you're choosing.

## 14. PORK CARNITAS

**Serving: 8**

**Preparation time: 7 hrs.15 min**

**Nutritional values: 442kcal Calories | 31g Fat | 9g Carbs30g Proteins**

## Ingredients

- 1 white, halved, and finely chopped onion
- Five cloves of garlic, chopped
- 1 jalapeño, chopped,
- 3 lbs. of cubed shoulder pork
- Salt and black pepper finely ground
- 1 tablespoon of cumin
- 2 tbsp. of fresh oregano minced
- Two Oranges
- 1 lemon
- 1/3 cup of broth of chicken

## Directions

1. At the base of a slow cooker, put the onion, jalapeño garlic, pork together. Add the salt, pepper, oregano & cumin.

2. The oranges and lime are zested over the pork, then halved, and the juice is squeezed over the pork. Also, spill the broth over the pork.

3. Put the cover on and adjust the heat to medium on the slow cooker. Process for 7 hours or unless the meat is soft and quick to squash with a fork.

4. Shred the pork with two forks. The pork may be eaten instantly or frozen in an airtight jar for up to 5 days in the fridge or for up to one month in the freezer.

# 15. CHICKEN MEATBALLS AND CAULIFLOWER RICE WITH COCONUT HERB SAUCE

PureWow

**Serving: 4**

**Preparation time: 45 minutes**

**Nutritional values: 205kcal calories | 13g Fat | 3g Carbs | 20g Proteins**

**Ingredients**

### For meatballs

- Non-stick spray
- 1 tablespoon of extra virgin olive oil
- 1/2 of the red onion
- 2 cloves of garlic, chopped

- 1 lb. of ground chicken
- 1⁄4 cup of finely minced parsley
- 1 tablespoon of Dijon mustard
- 3⁄4 tsp. of kosher salt
- 1⁄2 tsp. of freshly ground black pepper

## For sauce

- One 14-ounce of coconut milk can
- 11⁄4 cups of fresh, chopped parsley, distributed
- Four scallions, minced roughly
- 1 clove of garlic, peeled and crushed
- Juice and zest of one lime
- Kosher salt and black pepper, recently ground
- Red pepper flakes to serve.
- 1 Cauliflower Rice recipe

## Directions

1. **Prepare the meatballs:** Set the oven to 375°F. Cover a baking sheet with aluminum foil and coat it with a non-stick spray.

2. Heat the oil in a wide skillet over medium heat. Integrate the onion and simmer until soft, about five minutes. Integrate the garlic and simmer until tangy for around 1 minute.

3. Shift the onion and garlic to a mixing saucepan and let it cool completely. Mix in chicken, parsley, and mustard, sprinkle with salt. Turn the paste into 2 tablespoon balls and shift to the parchment paper.

4. Cook the meatballs for 17 to 20 minutes until firm and fully cooked.

5. **Prepare the sauce:** In a food processor pan, blend coconut milk, scallions, parsley, garlic, lime juice & lemon zest and stir unless buttery; season with salt and pepper.

6. Cover with the red pepper flakes as well as the leftover parsley. With the sauce, end up serving over the cauliflower rice.

## 16. KETO RAINBOW VEGGIES AND SHEET PAN CHICKEN

**Serving: 4**

**Preparation time: 40 minutes**

**Nutritional values: 380kcal Calories | 14g Fat | 35g Carbs | 31g Proteins**

**Ingredients**

- Spray for Nonstick
- 1 lb. of boneless chicken breasts without skin
- Sesame Oil 1 tbsp.

- 2 spoonful's of soy sauce
- Honey about 2 tablespoons
- 2 bell peppers, red, chopped
- 2 bell peppers yellow, chopped
- Three carrots, diced
- 1/2 broccoli head, sliced into cloves
- 2 red, chopped onions
- Extra virgin olive oil about 2 tablespoons
- Kosher salt and black pepper, recently ground
- 1/4 cup of fresh parsley, minced, for serving

## Directions

1. Heat up the oven to 400 degrees F. Slather a baking sheet lightly with non - stick spray.

2. Put the chicken on the baking tray. Stir the sesame oil and soy sauce together in a medium bowl. Dust the blend over the chicken equally.

3. On the baking dish, place the red and yellow bell peppers, broccoli, carrot & red onion. Sprinkle over the vegetables with olive oil and softly toss to coat; season with salt and pepper.

4. Roast it for 23 to 25 minutes until the veggies are soft and the chicken is thoroughly cooked. Take it out of the oven and seasoned it with parsley.

# 17. CAULIFLOWER POTATO SALAD

PureWow

**Serving: 6**

**Preparation time: 30-40 minutes**

**Nutritional values: 90kcal Calories | 4g Fat | 9g Carbs | 5g Proteins**

**Ingredients**

- 1 head cauliflower, sliced into chunks that are bite-sized
- 3⁄4 cup of Greek yogurt
- 1⁄4 cup of sour cream
- 1 tbsp. Mustard from Dijon
- 2 tbsp. apple cider vinegar
- 1 tablespoon of fresh parsley minced

- 1 tbsp. fresh dill minced
- Celery 4 stalks, finely chopped
- 1 bunch of green, finely chopped onions
- 1/3 cup of cornichons diced
- Kosher salt and black pepper, freshly processed

## Directions

1. Put the cauliflower, then coat it with water in a large container. Take the cauliflower to a simmer over moderate flame and boil until it is just fork soft, 8 to 10 minutes (do not overcook it, because, in the salad, it may not keep up).

2. Gently soak and cool the cauliflower to normal temperature. Meanwhile, mix the Greek yogurt, sour cream, mustard, vinegar, parsley, and dill together in a wide cup.

3. To incorporate, add the cauliflower, celery, green onions, and cornichons to the bowl and mix well. Sprinkle with salt & pepper.

4. When eating, chill the salad for a minimum of 1 hour. It is possible to prepare the salad 1 day in advance and keep it in the fridge until ready to eat.

# 18. PROSCIUTTO WRAPPED CAULIFLOWER BITES

**Serving: 8-10**

**Preparation time: 15 minutes**

**Nutritional values: 215kcal Calories | 15g Fat | 5g Carbs | 15g Proteins**

## Ingredients

- 1 tiny cauliflower
- 1/2 cup of paste of tomatoes
- 2 spoonful's of white wine
- 1/2 tsp. of black pepper
- 1/2 cup of Parmesan cheese grated
- 20 Prosciutto slices
- 6 tbsp. of extra-virgin olive oil

## Directions

1. Start preparing the cauliflower: Cut the base, and any green leaves, away from the cauliflower. Halve the cauliflower, and slice the halves into 1-inch-thick pieces. Based on the size of the slice, divide the slices into 2 or 3 bite-size bits.

2. Bring a big saucepan of salted water to a boil. In the water, parboil the cauliflower until almost soft, for 3 to 5 minutes. With paper towels, rinse the cauliflower well enough and pat off.

3. Add the tomato paste with the white wine & black pepper in a small dish to blend. On the edges of each slice of cauliflower, distribute 1 tsp., then dust with 1 tsp. of Parmesan. A prosciutto slice is carefully wrapped over each piece of cauliflower, pushing softly at the edge to seal it (it should twig well to the tomato-paste blend).

4. Continuing to work in chunks, heat two tablespoons of olive oil over moderate heat in a large pan. Add the cauliflower while the oil is hot and simmer unless the prosciutto is crispy and golden, 3 to 4 minutes on either side. Repeat till all the pieces are ready, with extra oil and cauliflower. Let it cool slowly, then serve right away.

# 19. CAULIFLOWER TORTILLAS

**Serving: 6**

**Preparation time: 45 minutes**

**Nutritional values: 45kcal Calories | 2g Fat | 5g Carbs | 4g Proteins**

**Ingredients**

- 1 head cauliflower
- 2 eggs, pounded lightly
- 1/2 tsp. cumin
- 1/4 tsp. of cayenne pepper
- Salt and black pepper, freshly processed, to taste

## Directions

1. Heat up the oven to 375°F. Use parchment paper to cover a baking sheet.

2. Split the cauliflower into thin strips. Cut the delicate portion of the stems roughly (discard the tough and leafy parts).

3. Move the cauliflower to the mixing bowl, filling it just halfway, working in bundles. Compress the cauliflower until it looks like rice, around 45 seconds to 1 minute. Repeat for the cauliflower that remains.

4. Move the cauliflower to a dish that is microwave-safe. Microwave around 1 minute, mix well, and microwave for an extra 1 minute.

5. Move the cauliflower to a tidy kitchen towel in the center. In a twist, cover the cauliflower up. Keep the towel over the basin and curl the ends to suck the humidity out of the cauliflower.

6. Take the cauliflower back to the bowl. Add the eggs, cumin, cayenne, salt, and black pepper, and mix well.

7. Ridge the lined baking sheet with 1/4 cup of cauliflower scoops. Distribute the cauliflower into 1/8-inch-thick circles using a tiny spoon.

8. For around 8 to 9 minutes, cook the tortillas until the bottoms are crispy. Then use a spatula to turn the tortillas over cautiously and cook for another 8 to 9 minutes unless crispy on the other side.

9. The tortillas can be eaten hot, instantly, or frozen for up to five days in an airtight jar in the fridge (with parchment pieces among them).

## 20. KETO SALMON SUSHI BOWL

**Serving: 3-4**

**Preparation time: 15 minutes**

**Nutritional values: 45kcal Calories | 6g Fat | 8g Carbs | 9g Proteins**

**Ingredients**

- Cauliflower Rice 3/4 Cup
- Smoked salmon about 1/2 packet
- 1/2 cup of cucumber spiraled
- Avocado 1/2
- 2 sheets of seaweed-dried
- 1 teaspoon of low sodium soy sauce
- Pepper & salt, to taste

- Wasabi 1/2 teaspoon, optional

**Sauce**

- 3 tbsp. mayonnaise
- Sriracha 1-2 teaspoon (adjust to preference)

**Direction**

1. Steam the cauliflower rice and incorporate salt and black pepper ( I used premade bag)
2. Put the rice layer with soy sauce as well as seasoning in the bottom of the small dish.
3. Fill the bowl with salmon, cucumber, seaweed, and avocado
4. Integrate mayo and Sriracha for sauce, adapting to the preferred heat.
5. Spread the sauce over a dish.
6. If desired, add sesame seeds as well as pepper for garnishing.

## 2.3 Keto Snacks

## 1. BAKED GARLIC PARMESAN ZUCCHINI CHIPS

**Serving: 6**

**Preparation time: 20-30 minutes**

**Nutritional values: 155kcal Calories | 10g Fat | 10g Carbs | 5g Proteins**

**Ingredients**

- Chopped 3 to 4 zucchini into pieces of 1/4-inch and 1/2-inch
- 3 tbsp. of Omega-3 DHA Extra Virgin Olive Oil STAR
- Salt to taste and freshly ground pepper
- 1 cup bread crumbs of panko

- 1/2- cup of Parmesan grated cheese
- 1 tsp. of oregano that is dried
- 1 tsp. of powdered garlic
- Cooking spray
- Non-Fat simple yogurt, for serving,

## Directions

1. Preheat the cooking oven to 450.

2. Line 3 foil-based baking sheets; brush lightly with cooking spray, then set it aside.

3. Incorporate the zucchini pieces, olive oil, salt, and pepper in a wide mixing bowl; whisk until well mixed.

4. Incorporate the crumbs, cheese, oregano, plus garlic powder in a different dish.

5. Dip the zucchini pieces in the cheese mixture and cover on both ends, press to remain with the coating.

6. On the prepared baking sheets, put the slices of zucchini in a thin layer.

7. Spray every slice lightly with cooking spray. This would help to achieve a texture that is crispier.

8. Flip the pan and finish frying for 8 - 10 mints, or until the chips are nicely browned — bake for ten min.

9. Remove it from the oven.

10. With Non-Fat Simple Yogurt, serve it.

# 2. KETO PIZZA ROLL-UPS

**Serving: 8-10**

**Preparation time: 15 minutes**

**Nutritional values: 138kcal Calories | 12g Fat | 8g Carbs | 6g Proteins**

**Ingredients**

- 12 mozzarella cheese slices
- Chunks of pepperoni, or you may use small pepperoni as well.
- Seasoning - Italian
- Marina Sauce - Keto

## Directions

1. Heat the oven to 400°F.

2. Using a baking mat and parchment paper, cover a cookie sheet.

3. Position the slices of cheese on the baking mat, then place them in the oven for 6 mints, or unless the slices of cheese tend to brown across the corners.

4. Take it out from the oven and leave to cool the cheese moderately. If you like, make the slices to chill and scatter with Italian seasoning, as well as include pepperoni.

5. With your chosen dipping sauce, wrap & serve! Enjoy

## 3. STUFFED MUSHROOMS WITH SAUSAGE

**Serving: 8**

**Preparation time: 30-40 minutes**

**Nutritional values: 280kcal Calories | 20g Fat | 6g Carbs | 15g Proteins**

**Ingredients**

- 1 pound of mild Italian sausage
- Cremini mushrooms about 1 pound
- 4 ounces of cream cheese
- 1/3 cup mozzarella - shredded
- Salt, as necessary
- ½ Teaspoon flakes of red pepper
- 1/4 cup of Parmesan grated cheese

**Directions**

1. To 350F, set the oven. Wash and cut the stems from the mushrooms.

2. Cook the sausage in a wide skillet over moderate heat. Transfer it to a wide mixing bowl until it has been cooked.

3. Add the mozzarella cheese, cream cheese, and mix to combine. Season to taste, then add salt & red pepper if required.

4. Spoon onto the mushroom caps with the sausage combination. Use Parmesan cheese for scattering. Put in a pan or casserole platter that is oven-safe.

5. Bake for 25 mints, unless the cheese is golden brown and the mushrooms are tender.

# 4. EASY KETO PIZZA BITES

**Serving: 30**

**Preparation time: 30-35 minutes**

**Nutritional values: 82kcal Calories | 7g Fat | 1g Carbs | 4g Proteins**

**Ingredients**

- 1 lb., cooked as well as drained Italian sausage
- Cream cheese, 4 ounces, softened.
- 1/3 of a cup of cocoa flour
- 1/2 tsp. powder for baking
- 1 tsp. of garlic diced

- 1 tsp. of seasoning - Italian
- 3 large, beaten eggs
- 1 1/4 cup mozzarella crushed

## Directions

1. Preheat the oven to 350°F.
2. Mix the prepared sausage & cream cheese unless fully fused together.
3. To give the flour time to ponder the moisture, rest of the ingredients until well mixed and cool for 10 minutes.
4. If you forget to chill the dough, they will deflate while they cook and will not be pleasant round balls.
5. Use a tiny cookie scoop to transfer onto a greased baking sheet (I prefer using the silicone baking mats).
6. Bake until lightly browned for 18-20 minutes.
7. This made 30, so it depends on the scale of the scoop you're using and how closely you're packing it.

# 5. CUCUMBER SLICES WITH HERB AND GARLIC CHEESE

**Serving: 16**

**Preparation time: 5 minutes**

**Nutritional values: 42kcal Calories | 3g Fat | 1g Carbs | 1g Proteins**

**Ingredients**

- 1 Diced English cucumber into 16 slices
- The Chives
- 6.5 ounces of Boursin or Alouette Herb & Garlic Cheese

**Directions**

1. To include some novelty, cut short slices of the cucumber skin with the help of a vegetable peeler.

2. Cut the cucumber to a thickness of around 1 mm.

3. Put the cheese in a pastry bag equipped with the edge of a large star.

4. The cucumber tips could clear every moister with a paper towel pat.

5. Puff each cucumber with the cheese and cover with a piece of chives.

## 6. KETO POPCORN - PUFFED CHEESE

**Serving: 5**

**Preparation: 10 minutes**

**Nutritional values: 80kcal Calories | 7g Fat | 0.3g Carbs | 5g Proteins**

**Ingredients**

- cheddar 100g/3.5 ounces

Directions

1. Slice the cheese into 0.5 inches / 1 cm pieces if you use diced cheddar. If you are using a block of cheddar, crush it to the same size using your fingertips.

2. Use a cloth/kitchen towel to wrap the cheese to keep it from being gritty and let it stay for up to 3 days in a hot, dry spot. You would like the cheese to be solid and dried absolutely.

3. Preheat oven to 390 Fahrenheit / 200 Celsius. On a baking tray covered with parchment paper, spread the cheese and bake for 4-five minutes before the cheese bursts. Put a new baking tray securely over the tray to keep it from popping out over the oven.

## 7. BACON WRAPPED BRUSSELS SPROUTS

**Serving: 4**

**Preparation time: 40 minutes**

**Nutritional values: 170kcal Calories | 15g Fat | 3g Carbs | 2g Proteins**

## Ingredients

12 bacon slices

12 Brussels sprouts, cut stems

Balsamic Dip:

Mayonnaise 5 tbsp.

Balsamic vinegar about 1 tbsp.

## Directions

1. Preparation: Set aside baking sheets and 12 toothpicks, covered with parchment paper or a baking mat that would be non-stick — preheat the baking oven to 400 F.

2. Wrap Sprouts: Put 1 slice of bacon on each sprout of Brussels, seal it with a toothpick, and put on the baking sheet in a thin layer.

3. Bake: Bake discovered at 400 F until the bacon is translucent and the Brussels are quite juicy around 40 minutes.

4. Serve: In a medium bowl, blend the mayonnaise & balsamic vinegar altogether unless creamy. Serve Brussels sprouts covered with bacon on a plate, along with the dip.

# 8. KETO ASPARAGUS FRIES

**Serving: 6**

**Preparation time: 1hour**

**Nutritional values: 202kcal Calories | 14g Fat | 7g Carbs | 14g Proteins**

**Ingredients**

- 1 pound of asparagus chopped (thick if possible)
- Salt and pepper to taste
- 1 cup of Parmesan cheese
- 3/4 cup of almond flour

- 1/4 tsp. of cayenne pepper
- 1/4 tsp. of baking powder
- 4 pounded eggs
- avocado oil spray

## Directions

1. Use a fork to cut the asparagus spikes with gaps — season well with a minimum of 1/2 teaspoon of salt. Put on paper towels and let it rest for 30 minutes.

2. In the meantime, mix 1 cup of Parmesan, cayenne pepper, almond flour & baking powder in a dish. Sprinkle with salt to taste.

3. Pound the egg in a different dish.

4. Soak the asparagus segments in the eggs, then cover with the blend of the cheese.

5. Your air fryer should be preheated to 400 degrees.

6. Organize the asparagus in one layer and, if required, cook in chunks. Spray the oil well — Cook for five minutes. Turn, and then respray.

7. Fry unless the asparagus is soft for the next 4 or 5 minutes.

# 9. EGG, BACON, AND CHEESE SLIDERS

**Serving: 6**

**Preparation time: 10 minutes**

**Nutritional values: 237kcal Calories | 18g Fat | 3g Carbs | 15g Proteins**

**Ingredients**

- 6 peeled, boiled eggs
- 6 Thin cheddar cheese strips

- 3 Slices of bacon that has been cooked
- 1/2 of Avocado
- 1/2 teaspoon Juice of a lime
- 1/2 Teaspoon cumin

## Directions

1. In a mixing bowl, place 1/2 of an avocado.
2. Stir in the cumin as well as lime juice. Mix until completely smooth. To taste, incorporate the salt.
3. Cut each hardboiled egg lengthwise in half.
4. Put on the lower half of the egg one piece of thinly cut cheddar cheese.
5. Place 1/2 a slice of cooked bacon on edge.
6. On the edge of the bacon, put a spoonful of the avocado mixture on top.
7. To make a little sandwich, place the remaining half of the egg face right over the top. Protect the bite of the egg with a toothpick placed down the center.
8. For your remaining eggs, replicate steps 4-7.
9. Add salt and pepper to each bite of the egg to taste & serve.

## 10. TURKEY BACON WRAP RANCH PINWHEELS

Joy Filled Eats

**Serving: 6**

**Preparation time: 15 minutes**

**Nutritional values: 133kcal Calories | 12g Fat | 2g Carbs | 5g proteins**

**Ingredients**

- 6 ounces of cheese cream
- 12 strips of smoked turkey deli (about 3 oz.)
- 1/4 teaspoon powdered garlic
- 1/4 teaspoon of chopped dried onion
- Dried dill weed 1/4 teaspoon
- 1 tablespoon of crumbling bacon

- 2 tablespoons cheddar shredded cheese

## Directions

1. Among 2 pieces of plastic wrap, place the cream cheese. Stretch it out until it's approximately 1/4 inch thick. Scrape the plastic wrap off the top piece. On top of the cream cheese, place the slices of turkey on the edge.

2. Cover and switch the whole item over with a fresh layer of plastic wrap. Chop off the plastic bit that is on the upper right now. Slather it on top of the cream cheese with the seasoning. Spray it with cheese and bacon.

3. Roll the pinwheels up such that the exterior is the turkey. Refrigerate for 2 minimum hours. On the edge of low-carb crackers or diced cucumber, cut into 12 bits and serve.

## 2.4 Keto Desserts

## 1. KETO BROWN BUTTER PRALINES

**Serving: 10**

**Preparation time: 16 minutes**

**Nutritional values: 338kcal Calories | 36g Fat | 3g Carbs | 2g Proteins**

**Ingredients**

- 2 Salted butter sticks

- Heavy cream 2/3 cup
- 2/3 Cup of Sweetener Granular 1/2 tsp. of xanthan gum
- 2 Cups Pecans diced
- Maldon Sea salt

## Directions

1. Use parchment paper or a silicone baking mat to make a cookie sheet.

2. Cook the butter in a skillet over medium flame, stirring regularly. It's going to take less than five min. Whisk in the heavy cream, sweetener, and xanthan gum. Extract it from the heat.

3. Mix in the nuts and put in the fridge, stirring regularly, for 1 hour to tighten up. The mixture's going to get really dense. Scrape onto the prepared baking sheet into 10 cookie styles and spray, if necessary, with the Maldon salt. Let the baking sheet freeze until frozen.

4. Store and keep stored in the fridge until served in an airtight dish.

## 2. KETO CHOCOLATE MOUSSE

**Serving: 4**

**Preparation time: 10 minutes**

**Nutritional values: 220kcal Calories | 25g Fat | 5g Carbs | 2g Proteins**

**Ingredients**

- 1 Cup of Whipped Heavy Cream
- 1/4 cup Cocoa powder unsweetened, sifted
- 1/4 Cup Sweetener Powdered
- 1 tsp. extract of vanilla
- Kosher salt about 1/4 teaspoon

**Directions**

1. Use the cream to whip into stiff peaks. Include the cocoa powder, vanilla, sweetener, and salt, then mix until all the products are mixed.

## 3. KETO CHEESECAKE FLUFF

**Serving: 6**

**Preparation time: 10 minutes**

**Nutritional values: 260kcal Calories | 27g Fat | 4g Carbs | 4g Proteins**

**Ingredients**

- 1 Cup of Whipping Heavy Cream

- 1 Eight oz. Cream Cheese Brick, Softened
- 1 Lemon Zest
- 1/2 Cup of Sweetener Granular

**Directions**

1. In a stand mixer, combine the heavy cream as well as stir until stiff peaks are made. A hand blender or a whisk can also be used by hand using a whisk.

2. In a different bowl, scrape the whipped cream and put it aside.

3. In the stand blender bowl, add the textured cream cheese, zest, and sweetener, then beat until sturdy.

4. With the cream cheese, add the whipped cream into the stand blender dish. Mix carefully until it is halfway mixed with a spatula. To finish whipping until sturdy, use the stand mixer.

5. Serve with a favorite topping of you.

# 4. LOW CARB BLUEBERRY CRISP

**Serving: 2**

**Preparation time: 20-25 minutes**

**Nutritional values: 390kcal Calories | 35g Fat | 17g Carbs | 6g Proteins**

**Ingredients**

- 1 Cup of Fresh or Frozen Blueberries
- 1/4 Cup Halves of Pecan
- Almond Meal/Flour 1/8 cup
- Butter around 2 tbsp.
- Granular Sweetener 2 tablespoons - distributed

- 1 tablespoon of flax
- Cinnamon 1/2 Teaspoon
- ½ teaspoon Extract from vanilla
- Kosher salt about 1/4 teaspoon
- Heavy cream 2 tablespoons

## Directions

1. Heat the oven to 400F.

2. Put 1/2 cup of blueberries and 1/2 tablespoons of swerve sweetener in 2, 1 cup ramekins. Blend and combine.

3. Incorporate the pecans, almond flour, butter, 1 tbsp. sweetener, cinnamon, ground flax, vanilla, and kosher salt into the food processor. Pulse while you mix the ingredients.

4. Place on top of the blueberries with the blend. Put the ramekins on a baking sheet and cook for 15-20 minutes in the middle of the oven or until the topping turn's toasty brown. Serve with 1 tablespoon of heavy cream slathered on top of each one.

# 5. 1 MINT LOW CARB BROWNIE

**Serving: 1**

**Preparation time: 3 minutes**

**Nutritional values: 196kcal Calories | 17g Fat | 2g Carbs | 8g Proteins**

**Ingredients**

- 2 tablespoons almond flour
- 1 tablespoon of preferred granulated sweetener
- 1 tablespoon powdered cocoa
- Baking Powder 1/8 teaspoon

- Almond butter 1 tablespoon. * See notes
- 3 tablespoons of milk, unsweetened almond milk,
- 1 tablespoon of chocolate chips of preference - optional

## Directions

1. A tiny microwave-protected cereal bowl or ramkin is lightly greased with cooking spray and placed aside.

2. Integrate all of your dried ingredients in a medium mixing bowl and blend well.

3. Integrate the creamy almond butter and milk in a separate bowl and mix them together. Place the wet and dry ingredients together and blend properly. Roll them through if chocolate chips are used.

4. Microwave at intervals of 30 seconds until the optimal texture has been reached. Take from the microwave then, before eating, let settle for one min.

# 6. KETO PEANUT BUTTER BALLS

Joy Filled Eats

**Serving: 18**

**Preparation time: 20 minutes**

**Nutritional values: 195kcal Calories | 17g Fat | 7g Carbs | 7g Proteins**

## Ingredients

- 1 cup of finely diced salted peanuts (not peanut flour)
- 1 cup of peanut butter
- 1 cup of sweetener powdered, like swerve
- 8-ounce chocolate chips free from sugar

## Directions

1. Combine the diced peanuts, peanut butter, and the sweetener, respectively. Distribute the 18-piece crust and mold it into balls. Put

them on a baking sheet covered with wax paper. Put it in the fridge until they're cold.

2. In the oven or on top of a dual boiler, heat the chocolate chips. Mix chocolate chips in the microwave, swirling every 30 seconds till they are 75percent melted. Then stir before the remainder of it melts.

3. Soak the chocolate for each peanut butter ball and put it back on the wax paper. Until the chocolate settles, put it in the fridge.

# 7. WHITE CHOCOLATE PEANUT BUTTER BLONDIES

**Serving: 16**

**Preparation time: 35 minutes**

**Nutritional values: 105kcal Calories | 9g Fat | 2g Carbs | 3g Proteins**

**Ingredients**

- 1/2 cup of peanut butter
- Softened butter around 4 tablespoons
- Two Eggs

- Vanilla 1 teaspoon
- 3 tbsp. fresh cocoa butter melted
- 1/4 cup of almond flour
- 1 tablespoon of coconut flour
- 1/2 cup sweetener
- 1/4 cup of fresh cocoa butter diced

## Directions

1. Preheat the baking oven to 350. Use cooking spray to cover the base of a 9 into 9 baking tray.

2. Beat the first 5 ingredients with an electric mixer until creamy. Bring the flour, sweetener, and sliced cocoa butter into the mixture. Scattered in a baking dish that has been prepared. Bake until the middle no longer jostles, and the corners are golden, for 25 minutes.

3. Cool thoroughly, and then, before slicing, chill in the freezer for 2-3 hours.

## 8. LOW CARB BAKED APPLES

**Serving: 4**

**Preparation time: 20 minutes**

**Nutritional values: 340kcal Calories | 88g Fat | 8g Carbs | 4g Proteins**

**Ingredients**

- 2 ounces. cheese,
- 1 oz. Walnuts or Pecans
- 4 tablespoon coconut flour
- Cinnamon 1/2 tsp.
- Vanilla extract around 1/4 teaspoon
- One tart/sour apple

**To serve**

- 3/4 cup of heavy whipped cream
- Vanilla extract about 1/2 teaspoon

**Directions**

1. Heat the oven to 175°C (350°F). In a crispy dough, mix the hot butter, diced almonds, coconut flour, cinnamon & vanilla together.

2. Wash the apple, but don't eliminate the seeds or chop it. Cut both edges off and cut 4 slices through the center portion.

3. In a greased baking dish, put the slices and place dough crumbs on top. Bake fifteen minutes or more or until light brown appears on the crumbs.

4. To a moderate bowl, incorporate heavy whipping cream as well as vanilla and whisk until soft peaks appear.

5. For a minute or two, let the apples chilled and serve with a spoonful of whipped cream.

# 9. FROZEN YOGURT POPSICLES

**Serving: 12**

**Preparation time: 10mins 2hours**

**Nutritional values: 73kcal Calories | 60g Fat | 28g Carbs | 13g Proteins**

## Ingredients

- 8 oz. Mango chilled, chopped
- 8 oz. Strawberries chilled
- 1 cup of Greek full-fat yogurt
- 1/2 cup of heavy whipped cream
- 1 teaspoon extract of vanilla

## Directions

1. Let the strawberries and mango defrost for 10 to 15 minutes.
2. In a mixer, place all the materials and combine until creamy.
3. End up serving as fluffy ice cream instantly or pipe into Popsicle shapes and chill for at least a few hours. If you do have an ice cream machine, it can be used, of course.

# 10. CHOCOLATE AVOCADO TRUFFLES

**Serving: 20**

**Preparation time: 35 minutes**

**Nutritional values: 65kcal Calories | 76g Fat | 19g Carbs | 5g Proteins**

**Ingredients**

- 1 (7 ounces.) ripe, diced avocado
- Vanilla extract about 1/2 teaspoon
- 1/2 lemon, zest
- About 1 pinch of salt
- Five ounces. Dark chocolate containing cocoa solids of at least 80 percent, finely diced
- 1 spoonful of coconut oil
- 1 tbsp. cocoa powder unsweetened

**Directions**

1. Use an electric mixer to mix the avocado and vanilla extract. The use of ripe avocado is necessary in order for the mixture to be fully creamy.

2. Add a tablespoon of salt and mix in the lemon zest.

3. In boiling water or oven, melt the chocolate & coconut oil.

4. Incorporate the chocolate & avocado and blend properly. Let it rest for 30 minutes in the fridge or until the batter is compact but not fully solid.

5. With your fingertips, shape little truffle balls. Likewise, use two teaspoons or a tiny scoop. Morph and roll in the cocoa powder with the hands.

## 11. CRUNCHY KETO BERRY MOUSSE

**Serving: 8**

**Preparation time: 10 minutes**

**Nutritional values: 256kcal Calories | 26g Fat | 3g Carbs | 2g Proteins**

**Ingredients**

- Two cups of heavy whipped cream
- Three ounces. Fresh strawberries or blueberries or raspberries
- 2 oz. Pecans diced
- 1/2 of a lime, zest
- Vanilla extract around 1/4 teaspoon

## Directions

1. Drop the cream into a container and whip until soft peaks appear using a hand mixer. Towards the top, add the lime zest, then vanilla.

2. Cover the whipped cream with berries & nuts and stir thoroughly.

3. Wrap with plastic and allow for 3 or even more hours for a stable mousse to settle in the fridge. While you don't like a less firm consistency, you can also experience the dessert instantly.

# Conclusion

Ketogenic' is a name for a diet that is low-carb. The concept is for you to obtain more protein and fat calories and fewer carbs. You reduce much of the carbs, such as sugar, coffee, baked goods, and white bread that are easily digestible.

If you consume fewer than 50 g of carbs a day, the body can gradually run out of resources (blood sugar) that you can use instantly. Usually, this takes 3 or 4 days. Then you're going to start breaking down fat and protein for nutrition, which will help with weight loss. This is classified as ketosis.

A ketogenic diet plan intended to induce ketosis, disintegrate body fat into ketones and enable the body to perform on ketones instead of glucose to a great extent. Since samen is the ultimate aim of these diets, there are typically a lot of connections between the various forms of the ketogenic diet, especially in terms of being low in carbohydrates and high in dietary fat. A program that focuses on high-fat and low carbohydrates is the Ketogenic Diet, and it has many advantages.

It is necessary to remember that a short-term diet that emphasizes weight reduction rather than medical benefits is a ketogenic diet. To reduce weight, people use a keto diet more commonly, although it may help treat some medical problems, such as epilepsy, too. People with heart problems, some neurological disorders, and also acne can even be supported, although further research in those fields needs to be conducted.

# Intermittent Fasting for Women Over 50

*The Winning Formula to Lose Weight, Unlock Your Metabolism and Rejuvenate Above 50's*

*[13 Anti-Aging Tips Included]*

**By**

**Alessandro Vasquez**

# Table of Contents

# Disclaimer

This book is not a substitute for medical advice. All information and tools presented within this text are intended for motivational purposes.

Any health, diet or exercise advice shared here is not intended as medical diagnosis or treatment. If you think you have any type of medical condition you must seek professional advice even if you believe it may be due to diet, food or exercise. You should always consult a qualified practitioner before using any dietary, exercise or health advice from this text.

# INTRODUCTION

## THE BENEFITS OF FASTING

Fasting is not something that most of us ever think about – food is everywhere and, in all likelihood, right now you're within striking distance of an emergency skinny latte and a muffin. Now I love food as much as the next person, so what I find great about fasting is that it's as much about eating delicious things as it is about abstaining. And there are none of the harmful effects you get from following crazy diets or popping pills, because fasting provides a natural high, an inner boost that works with your body, not against it.

When I first learned about fasting, it was in the context of an invitation to join an intensive meditation retreat in the Himalayas. In fact, I only stumbled across meditation in a foggy, end-of-yoga-class kind of way (and usually ended up snoring!). By contrast, I'd always been fascinated by the inner poise of people who did yoga. I didn't just envy their lithe bodies – I wanted their unshakable contentment and smiling eyes. How did they manage to waft around so effortlessly and have boundless energy for eye-watering yoga moves? And they all seemed to look incredibly youthful and naturally glowing. What was their secret? Whatever it was, I had to have it. So, as you do when you are childless and too young to care about a job and responsibilities, I gave up a regular salary and sold my worldly possessions to enjoy an alternative (and rather late) gap year in an Indian ashram where I planned to study yoga and meditation. Admittedly, it was the thought of becoming supple and slender rather than discovering nirvana that sweetened the deal for me. As it happened, one of the simplest techniques I learned over those intensive months has become one of my most important life lessons for mind and body – how to fast.

Fasting is so easy; you really can't fail. In fact, it's something we all do already – breakfast, quite literally, is breaking a fast of around 12 hours. And let's not forget one of the best things of all – if you "do" fast properly (there are several techniques to choose from and by the end of the book you will discover which one suits you), you can finally give up on the endless hamster wheel of weight loss and gain that sees otherwise sane and successful people becoming slaves to whatever dieting fad happens to be the flavor of the month. I know the pain of that world because I existed in it for so long. I also know how good it feels to be free of it.

# FASTING VERSUS OTHER WEIGHT-LOSS APPROACHES

It's time to stick my neck out. I'd go as far to say that I see fasting as the future of weight loss. The diet industry is just that – an industry – and a great many consumers have woken up to the fact that they have been sold a dummy. As any seasoned dieter knows, behind the hype and celebrity following, many trendy diet plans are just plain silly and impractical.

Long-term calorie restriction, the backbone of traditional weight loss, can make you prone to weight gain. Not only that, the nutritional aspects of many commercially savvy weight-loss plans are at best borderline, and at worst downright dangerous. The fact that one of the largest dieting companies in the world is owned by a confectionery company illustrates (to me at least) that the industry behind dieting and the promise of weight loss may need a bit of a shake-up.

Fundamentally, fasting for weight loss is all about nutrition. When you do eat, you must eat well. When you're fasting, there's no cutting out of major food groups such as carbohydrates or essential fats. In this book you'll find lots of information about what to eat when you adopt a fasting regime, rather than simply calculating when you don't eat. In fact, nutrition is even more important when you're fasting since you're eating less overall.

If I'm right and fasting becomes the next big thing in dieting, what will happen? Well, fasting is already rapidly gaining in popularity and when a trend begins – particularly a global trend – newspaper headlines don't necessarily get all the facts right. And when a trend imbibes the collective consciousness, particularly in weight loss, you can guarantee that money-wasting gimmicks will follow. Therefore, as part of your induction into the world of fasting, I'll be giving you a gimmick-free tour of the scientifically backed benefits of fasting for weight loss, longevity and performance.

Every piece of advice in this book is sound and practical. In my research I've discovered that in order to achieve the best results, fasting techniques should be subtly different for women and men, and different again if you're using fasting to enhance performance. Whilst science acts as the perfect signpost, we're all unique – biologically, physically and emotionally, and ultimately it remains your job and your job alone to turn evidence into action.

Even with the greatest advances, there are certain things that science, or nutrition for that matter, can't explain fully but I will nevertheless attempt to describe how fasting may make you feel more connected and happier in yourself. Fasting, more than any other nutrition or diet approach, can help you to reset your attitude and recognize the difference between physical hunger and appetite. Slowing down your eating can make the experience as much a "mental break" as a physical boost. Indeed, fasting has been used for centuries as a method of mental and spiritual purification. It's like setting a part of you free again.

# THE SCIENCE ON FASTING

The scientific studies on fasting focus largely on alternate-day fasting and on prolonged periods of fasting. Much of the scientific research is done on animals rather than on humans – mainly because it's considered unethical to starve people for no reason! However, the evidence that is out there about the benefits of fasting is just so compelling and exciting that it's worthy of a few minutes of your attention (and I'll be busting several dieting myths along the way).

The following are a few highlights from the science of fasting that we'll explore in the forthcoming chapters:

## FASTING FOR WEIGHT LOSS

- It might seem counter-intuitive, but intermittent fasting could help you get your hunger under control. This is partly because of its effects on your hunger hormones, and partly because it helps you to learn the difference between physical and emotional hunger.
- Forget what you've been told about regular meals boosting metabolism – studies show that people who are overweight tend to snack more often.
- Fasting is just as effective as traditional diets for losing weight, but might be easier to stick to and less likely to slow your metabolism – perfect if you want to lose that last bit of stubborn flesh.
- If you're stressed, and troubled by weight around your middle, shorter fasts may be better at tackling belly fat than longer ones.

# FASTING FOR HEALTH

- Fasting – especially in combination with eating less protein – acts like a "spring clean" for the body by switching on a cellular mechanism called autophagy and by reducing the levels of a hormone called insulin-like growth factor (IGF-1) that can send cell growth out of control.

- Regular juice fasts may deliver potent anti-ageing benefits without you having to cut out food completely.

- Whichever fasting format you choose, it's likely to reduce inflammation – good news for conditions such as eczema, asthma and arthritis.

- Contrary to the popular belief that sugary snacks are "brain food", fasting may help adults to concentrate better. It could even help to build new brain cells.

# FASTING FOR WOMEN

- The effects on blood sugar control seem to be different in women and men. Studies suggest that fasting improves men's blood sugar control, but may not have a beneficial effect on women.

- Most women know that adopting any new healthy habit is generally more challenging the week before their period starts. So, my advice is to go easy that week. Your nearest and dearest will be thankful too.

- When it comes to the overall impact of fasting on menstrual cycles, we only have animal studies to go on, and the effects aren't clear. However, any improvements in overall diet usually go some way to helping with any menstrual problems – so make sure you pay as much attention to what you do eat as you do to what you don't eat. If you notice any negative changes, or have lost weight to the point where your periods become disrupted, stop fasting.

## FASTING FOR GYM BUNNIES

- Doing weight training while fasting can help your body build more muscle.
- If you favor cardio workouts, training while fasting can help your body learn to tap into its fat stores more intensively – but it's not such a good idea to run a race without eating beforehand.
- Again, there are gender differences – men tend to build muscle so long as they work out before their main meal, whereas women seem to respond better to training after a meal.

# Part 1

## Knowledge (The Winning Formula to Lose Weight)

## Chapter One

## EAT, FAST AND LOSE WEIGHT

Fasting simply means extending the time between meals when we don't eat, and is something that humans have practiced since they first walked the planet. It's only in recent times that we've had access to food 24 hours a day. Before then, we typically went for extended periods without eating. Fasting's no passing "fad" – unlike the modern trend of "grazing", the notion that we should constantly be ingesting small amounts. Interest in when and what we eat and drink has been increasing steadily and is set to continue. Nutritional knowledge helps us understand how our bodies and minds work, and nutritional intervention has a major role to play in the lives of everyone, from Olympic athletes to busy mums and people with medical conditions. No longer seen as something "alternative", nutritional therapy has now gone mainstream.

## FASTING TODAY

Celebrities are usually the first to focus attention on any technique that involves the body beautiful, and fasting is no exception. So, as part of my research for this book, I went in search of some of the world's most famous celebrity personal trainers to ask them if they use fasting with their clients.

I've used intermittent fasting on many occasions – notably when people need to lose those last 2–4.5kg [5–10lb], or in order to stimulate stubborn fat loss. I have one client who fasts every Wednesday, just drinks water, green tea, some amino acids, and that's it, and that works very well for her. There are many protocols for fasting and each individual can use the one that works best for them. As with all diets though, the protocol needs to be sustainable so it can be implemented into a lifestyle."

If you still believe that fasting is just another passing diet fad – here today, gone tomorrow – think again. As I mentioned in the Introduction, I predict that fasting will not only become the next big global health trend but that it's here to stay. From a professional point of view, a technique that gets results without compromising health, that helps restore a sense of calm in the mind, and that costs nothing to do, kind of has it all.

## THE TRUTH ABOUT FAT AND WEIGHT LOSS

These days, in countries where there's an abundance of food, we've become used to constant grazing – rarely sitting down for meals and simply picking at high-calorie, high-fat and high-sugar foods all day long. We've forgotten what it feels like to be really physically hungry.

The unfortunate truth is that many of us are designed to get fat. It all comes down to evolution. Back in the dim and distant past, when food shortages were common, people who had substantial fat "in storage" were more likely to survive.

Research carried out in the last century proved that extended periods of starvation are much less dangerous for people who have high levels of body fat – in fact, the heavier you are, the more likely it is that fasting will lead to substantial fat loss with muscle being spared. In contrast, the slimmer you are (and your ancestors were), the more likely it is that you'll break down muscle through extreme dieting.

People often blame their genes for a "slow metabolism" or "big bones", but it turns out things are more complicated than that. The genetic factors that helped your ancestors lay down fat stores seem to relate to a complex range of factors rather than simply affecting your metabolic rate. For example, there are subtle differences in appetite, or in the tendency to fidget.

## WHY SOME PEOPLE ARE NATURALLY SLIM

Emerging research suggests that naturally slim people have genetic advantages that make it easier for them to avoid weight gain. They're not blessed with faster metabolisms, but tend to be able to regulate their appetite and burn off excess calories without even noticing it.

## TO THEM, FOOD IS JUST FOOD

Naturally slim people enjoy food, but they don't have a strong emotional connection to it. Foods aren't "good" or "bad", they're just food. Therefore, slim types don't feel guilty when they tuck into a slice of cake or have a few chips with their dinner.

## THEY CAN STOP AFTER JUST ONE BITE

When our naturally slim friends eat indulgent foods, they can stop after just a little, rather than polishing off the plate. Many of us are familiar with that feeling of having broken the diet rules:

"That's today ruined… I may as well finish the whole cake and start again tomorrow."

Slim people don't get that "all-or-nothing" feeling that's typical in seasoned dieters.

## THEY RECOGNIZE THE DIFFERENCE BETWEEN HUNGER AND APPETITE

The mechanisms controlling our appetites are complex. Research suggests that naturally slim people may be more resistant to appetite signals that aren't linked to physiological hunger. What this means is, they eat when their body needs nourishment, not when their brain is trying to trick them into believing they're hungry. In contrast, those of us with a genetic tendency to gain weight can feel physically hungry when tempted by food, even if our bodies don't need the calories.

## THEY BURN IT OFF

There's a theory that our body weight has a "set point" (a natural weight at which it tries to maintain itself). When a naturally slim person overeats, they tend to compensate by moving around more, without even thinking about it. So, as well as a few more gym sessions, they may fidget, get stuck into cleaning the house, or walk rather than taking the car. But for the majority of us, overeating is followed by a few hours relaxing on the sofa!

## OTHER FACTORS INFLUENCING WEIGHT

Ultimately, weight gain comes down to the fact that we're eating more calories than we're burning off, and over time this has led to many of us gradually getting fatter. But tackling the issue is about more than simply cutting calories. The quality of what we eat is important too. The types of food that are so readily available to us – those muffins and sugary drinks – tend to be packed with sugar or refined carbohydrates (carbs) and it's very easy to eat them and not notice when we're full. Instead, try replacing those "empty" calories with nutrient-rich, lean proteins, leafy green vegetables and even healthy fats from nuts and oily fish. I promise you; these will make you feel full and you'll be much less tempted to overeat.

It's also important to detect underlying problems or habits that can be causing or contributing to a weight problem. For example, stress, emotional eating or chemical calories may have been the tipping point for your body. Unhealthy eating can mean that you're not getting enough of the vitamins, minerals and essential fats that your body needs to function well. What's more, many "fad" diets aren't nutritionally balanced, so they starve the body of the vital nutrients your body needs.

On a basic level, these problems can make it very hard for you to stick to a diet. Likewise, "crash" diets tend to drastically restrict your body's intake of calories. If your body isn't getting the nutrients it needs, the result can be irritability, depression and even lowered brain function, all of which inevitably affect your motivation to continue with the diet. And when you come off the diet, you quickly return to your previous weight and may end up gaining even more weight. This is because, when you lose weight, your metabolic rate naturally dips – more about this shortly.

## STRESS AND WEIGHT GAIN

The link between stress and weight gain begins with tiny glands called adrenals. Their basic task is to rush all your body's resources into "fight or flight" mode by increasing production of adrenaline and other hormones – you may recognize this feeling with an increased heart rate, and your blood pressure may be raised.

Unlike our ancestors, who weren't distracted by mobile phones, deadlines, emails and the multi-tasking challenges of modern life, today we live under constant stress. Instead of occasional, acute demands followed by rest, we're constantly over-worked, under-nourished, exposed to environmental toxins, and plagued by worries… with no let-up.

Every challenge to the mind and body creates a demand on the adrenal glands. The result is a state of constant high alert and high levels of the hormone cortisol in the body, leading to a huge number of health problems, such as a tendency to hold on to stubborn belly fat. The other main side- effects of stress and adrenal overload are digestive problems, rapid ageing, lowered immunity and skin problems.

Sometimes it's less about the stress in our lives and more about the stress we place on ourselves with what we eat and drink. Take caffeine, for example. We're all familiar with the "buzz" that caffeine can give. Many products are marketed solely on the basis of this false energy kick, but that lively feeling is actually the sensation of adrenaline being pumped around the body as a result of the caffeine hit. The adrenal glands tire of constant stimulation and when the inevitable adrenal fatigue kicks in, it leads to a slowdown in the conversion of stored fats (and proteins and carbohydrates) into energy. We experience this failure in the energy chain as a craving for further stimulants in the form of more caffeine from another cup of tea, coffee, cola drink or caffeinated beverage. The last piece of the picture with caffeine is what usually comes with it. Remember that an average coffee these days contains a sizeable portion of milk, sugar or syrup and then there's the ubiquitous temptation of a muffin or pastry accompaniment!

## INSULIN RESISTANCE AND THE EFFECTS OF ALCOHOL

When the body is overloaded with carbs (which are extremely commonplace in the average Western diet), it has to respond by making more insulin. Carbs are broken down into molecules of the sugar glucose, and insulin is the hormonal "key" that unlocks the cells to allow the glucose in. Over a period of time, excess insulin affects the cells by making them less sensitive to taking sugars into the cell and creating energy. This in turn prevents the cells from burning fat. The good news is that fasting may improve how your body handles sugar and help your body burn fat instead of storing it.

As far as your body's concerned, alcohol is chemically similar to sugar, so drinking any form of alcohol will set off the same insulin resistance seesaw that can promote weight gain. And that's before you even begin to consider the calorie content of the drink itself, which is likely to be very high and devoid of any nutritional benefit – so-called "empty calories". What's more, alcohol acts as a potent appetite booster, so more alcohol equals more food consumed!

There's yet another reason behind alcohol's "beer belly" effect. Alcohol reduces the amount of fat your body burns for energy, while preventing the absorption of many of the essential nutrients needed for successful weight loss, particularly the B vitamins and vitamin C. In one study published in the American Journal of Clinical Nutrition, eight men were given two glasses of vodka with diet lemonade, each containing just under 90 calories. For several hours after drinking the vodka, the amount of fat the men burned dropped by a massive 73 percent. Because your body uses more than one source of fuel, if alcohol is consumed then this alcohol "energy" will be used instead of fat – not good news for the waistline!

## EMOTIONAL EATING

As we all know, a lot of eating is emotionally driven. Many people with weight problems fear feeling hungry. Furthermore, reaching for the sugar-fix from food or from alcohol is what helps free us, temporarily, from whatever uncomfortable emotion we might be feeling. Of course, sometimes an eating problem masks an underlying psychological problem or challenge. In such cases, expert advice, counselling or psychotherapy or psychology can really help.

Even when eating is free from emotional factors, the fact is, the longer you spend on a diet (whether for health or for weight loss), the less strict you become and the more likely it is that calories will sneak in without you noticing – a bite of this here, a nibble of that there. Fasting shakes up this model of eating altogether. Having a large section of the day when food simply isn't allowed to pass your lips prevents random snacking, and might also alert you to how often you do this normally. If you'd describe yourself as someone with limited self- control, fasting is an easier option than almost any other diet out there as you don't have to count every calorie or become a slave to food group fads – the only thing you really need to do is watch the clock.

## "CHEMICAL CALORIES"

It's thought that chemicals in the environment have a blocking effect on the hormones that control weight loss. When the brain is affected by these toxins, hormone signaling can be impaired. Reducing chemicals in our homes, foods and drinks is important when looking at the overall picture of weight loss and health. As you'll discover in the "Nutritional Rules for Fasting" chapter, one of my nutrition rules as part of any fasting program me is to eat real food rather than fake food. If you can't pronounce what it says on the label, you probably shouldn't be eating it!

## THYROID PROBLEMS

An underactive thyroid can cause weight gain, too. Symptoms include fatigue, cold, hormonal problems, depression and low libido as well as unexplained weight gain. The challenge is sometimes that the problem is sub- clinical, in other words, your test from the doctor may come back negative but you still have the symptoms. This can be frustrating for the sufferer as it sometimes means a re-visit in six months to a year to see if the symptoms register as qualifying for medical intervention.

A nutritious diet designed with thyroid health in mind can help. For the thyroid to work optimally, it needs nutrients such as iodine, manganese, vitamin C, methionine, magnesium, selenium, zinc, and the amino acids cysteine and L-tyrosine. These are all found in healthy foods such as fruit, vegetables, nuts, seeds and meat.

# WHY TRADITIONAL DIETING MAKES YOU HUNGRY

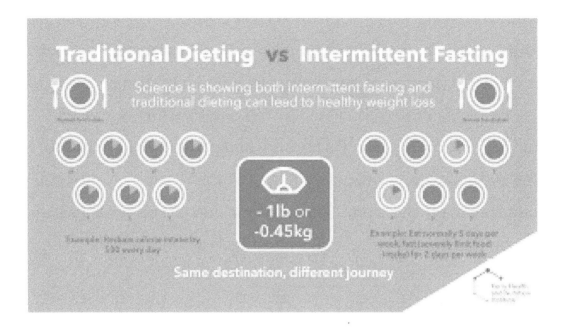

Going on a traditional diet without adequate energy intake for long periods of time can make your metabolic rate plummet and your appetite soar. Say you reduce your calories to below 1,000 a day for a number of weeks to fit into a party dress, the chances are you'll feel hungry and fed up much of the time, and as soon as the party starts, you'll dive head first into all the foods you've been avoiding, re-gaining that lost weight in no time! This, in a nutshell, sums up the seesaw of the diet industry.

The real trick is to keep your body feeling fuller for longer. I'm not talking about choosing one ready-meal over another, it's about understanding how to manage hunger so you naturally eat less most of the time. Please note, I don't say all of the time. Special events and over-indulging every now and then are good for the soul.

In tandem with a good diet overall, fasting can be used to retrain your hunger without the need for appetite suppressants or dodgy supplements. When you begin to fast, you will feel hungry at your usual meal times. However, if you choose not to eat at that time, the peaks and troughs of hunger start to level out. All this happens without a decrease in metabolic rate. It doesn't take a genius to recognize that if you feel hungry less often, you'll eat less and therefore lose weight. There's a biological explanation for this. Feelings of hunger and satiety (feeling full) are controlled by two main hormones produced within the body, ghrelin (even the word sounds hungry) and leptin. This dynamic duo of hormones has a powerful effect on how much food you eat and how much of what you've consumed you "burn off".

## GHRELIN

This hormone seems pretty straightforward. When your stomach's empty, it sends out some ghrelin to tell an area of your brain, the hypothalamus, that you ought to be eating. You then feel ravenous. But research published in the American Journal of Physiology suggests that ghrelin levels also rise in anticipation of eating – you get hungry partly because you're expecting a meal, not just because you have an empty stomach.

On a traditional diet, you get a peak of ghrelin before every meal – but because you don't eat as much as you'd really like to, you never feel fully satisfied. When you're fasting, your ghrelin levels still rise, but anecdotal evidence suggests that over time your body finds this sensation easier to get used to, probably because of the changes in your meal patterns. There's also a theory that a nutritionally poor diet sends ghrelin rocketing faster than a nutrient-dense plan like the ones I recommend.

# WHY MOST DIETS FAIL

This probably isn't the first book about weight loss you've ever read. I often say I've been down the diet road myself so many times that I could be a tour guide. If you're asking yourself why fasting is going to be any different, here are the facts you need to know:

• "Yo-yo" dieting is the bane of many people's lives, but even if you've lost and gained weight countless times, recent research has shown that it's possible to lose weight safely without messing up your metabolism.

• Burning off more calories than you eat is the only way to lose weight – and the simple truth is that you will lose weight if you manage to keep the number of calories you eat below the amount you burn off… boring but true.

There are hundreds of different ways to create a calorie deficit – as evidenced by the huge diet book, diet shake, diet bar and "miracle" weight-loss supplement industry. But there are two main reasons why diets never tend to live up to their expectations, especially as you get closer to your goal weight:

1    Traditional diet misrepresent the calories in/calories out equation.

We've all heard that 450g (1lb) of fat is roughly equal to 3,500 calories, so the traditional calorie-counting approach is to cut calories by 500–1,000 per day in order to lose 450–900g (1–2lb) per week. The trouble is, as you get slimmer you become lighter and that actually reduces the number of calories you burn at rest (your basal metabolic rate). So, in traditional weight-loss plans, weight loss is initially rapid but tends to slow down over time, even if you maintain that original calorie deficit. This can be very demotivating.

## 2 It's sticking to your chosen approach that's often the hard part.

Even if you get your calories exactly right, how boring does counting every calorie get? Demotivation – either as a result of not seeing the numbers on the scales going down as quickly as they were, or boredom – can lead to lapses, which slow down the rate of weight loss even further. When you go back to your old eating habits – surprise, surprise – you'll gain all the weight back, and a little more, as a result of the natural dip in basal metabolic rate (calorie burn) caused by your initial weight loss.

# HOW FASTING MAKES A DIFFERENCE

## FASTING MAY BOOST METABOLIC RATE

You're probably thinking, "If I start starving myself, won't that be worse for my metabolism?" First of all, fasting is not starving yourself, and don't worry that eating less often will damage your metabolism. Losing weight naturally slows your basal metabolic rate (the number of calories you burn at rest) in proportion to the amount of weight you lose, no matter which method you use. This is because your daily energy (calorie) needs are directly related to your age, height, gender and weight, in particular your lean body mass (muscle). It doesn't mean that eating more often will fire up your metabolism.

You'll hear over and over again that after a night of sleep, your metabolism has ground to a halt and you need to eat breakfast to stoke your metabolic fire. The idea that "breakfast boosts metabolism" is simply not true – it hasn't been backed up by research at all. The breakfast myth is based on the "thermic effect of food". Around 10 percent of our calorie burn comes from the energy that we use to digest, absorb and assimilate the nutrients in our meals. Roughly speaking, if you eat a 350-calorie breakfast, you'll burn 35 calories in the process. But notice that you've eaten 315 extra calories to burn that 35. No matter what time of day you eat, you'll burn off around 10 percent of the calories in your food through the thermic effect of food. So, whether you eat your breakfast at 7am, 10am or never, if you eat roughly the same amount and types of food overall, its effect on your metabolism will be the same.

In fact, all the research on fasting seems to show that eating less often could actually boost your metabolic rate. In one British study conducted at the University of Nottingham, a two-day fast boosted participants' resting metabolic rate by 3.6 percent. In another study by the same research group, 29 healthy men and women fasted for three days. After 12–36 hours, there was a significant increase in basal metabolic rate, which returned to normal after 72 hours. The exact mechanisms for why this happens aren't clear.

# FASTING INCREASES FAT BURN

What is clear is that more of the calories you use for fuel during fasting come from your fat stores. Scientists can estimate what proportion of your energy is coming from fats and carbohydrates by measuring the amount of oxygen inhaled and the amount of carbon dioxide exhaled in your breath. The higher the proportion of oxygen to carbon dioxide, the more fat you're burning. As part of the same Nottingham study, findings proved that the proportion of energy obtained from fat rose progressively over 12–72 hours, until almost all the energy being used was coming from stored fat. This is incredible news really!

We're so often told to "breakfast like a king, lunch like a prince and dine like a pauper" with a view to becoming healthy, wealthy and wise. This is usually explained by telling us that breakfast kick-starts the metabolism – but it turns out that eating breakfast doesn't boost your fat-burning potential at all. In a small study on breakfast-eaters – published in the British Journal of Nutrition – a 700-calorie breakfast inhibited the use of fat for fuel throughout the day. Put simply, when we eat carbohydrates, we use it for fuel, and this prevents our bodies tapping into our stubborn stored fat. Constant grazing might be what's keeping fat locked away in your belly, bum or thighs – and fasting is one way to release it.

## FASTING MAINTAINS LEAN MUSCLE

The more muscle you have, the more calories you burn at rest. And before you say you don't want big muscles, another way to put that is: the less muscle you lose as you drop in weight, the less your basal metabolic rate falls as you move toward your goal weight. (Remember, your basal metabolic rate is the rate at which you burn calories, so it's really important in order to make staying in shape easier in the long term.) Besides, muscle takes up less room than fat. So, a person with good lean muscle mass will take a smaller dress size or use a narrower belt notch than someone who doesn't have it.

Fasting is better than plain old calorie restriction when it comes to maintaining lean body mass. This is largely because fasting triggers the release of growth hormone (GH), which encourages your body to look for other fuel sources instead of attacking its muscle stores. This is thought to be a survival advantage – back when humans were hunter gatherers it wouldn't have made sense for our muscle mass to reduce when food was scarce – we needed strong legs and arms to hunt down our dinner!

In one study carried out by researchers at Intermountain Medical Center in the USA, participants were asked to fast for 24 hours. During this time, GH levels rose by a whopping 1,300 percent in women and 2,000 percent in men.

It's important to note that more isn't necessarily better when it comes to GH – what's key is resetting the balance between GH release (which happens in the fasted state) and insulin release (which happens in the fed state, however small your meal) in order to stimulate fat loss without losing lean muscle. You never need to fear growing giant muscles as a result of fasting – GH is released in waves and goes back to normal levels quickly as soon as your body has released enough fat to burn.

As mentioned earlier, if you're already slim, it's especially important not to overdo it when fasting. Research published in the academic journal Obesity Research shows that within just two days of complete fasting, there's a dramatic increase in the use of muscle for fuel in people who are already a healthy weight. This is because they have less fat available to burn overall. Perhaps the advice for people who are already svelte but who want to fast for health benefits is to fast little and often rather than to eat little and often.

## FASTING PATTERNS GIVE YOU ENERGY WHEN YOU NEED IT

Alongside maintaining your muscle mass to reduce the dip in your metabolic rate that happens as you lose weight, fasting may help with stubborn weight in other ways.

There's a theory that the reduction in calorie burn typically seen after following a calorie-restricted diet may be related more to changes in activity level than to basal metabolic rate. When you're only eating, say, 1,200 calories day after day, it may be difficult to maintain the energy levels and motivation to exercise. But following an intermittent fasting pattern means that you can concentrate your workouts around the times when you're eating. More energy means a tougher workout – and more calorie burn overall.

# COMMON QUESTIONS AND ANSWERS

**Q**    Isn't "not eating" dangerous?

**A**    It's very important to establish that fasting is not starvation, which, of course, is dangerous. What I'm talking about is the health benefits of increasing the gaps between meals or eating less from time to time.

Some people who are fully signed up to the merry-go-round of traditional dieting will argue that not eating is likely to induce a low-blood-sugar or "hypo" episode. Feeling faint, clammy and unable to concentrate are typical symptoms, happily offset by a visit to the vending machine or, for the health- aware, a snack such as an oatcake or nuts and seeds. I'm not suggesting that snacking should be outlawed – most of the time, I'm more than happy to tuck right in. But fasting challenges the assertion that we can't survive, or even thrive, without five mini-meals a day.

**Q**    Won't I feel light-headed and really hungry on a fast?

**A**    You might be worried that your blood sugar levels will dip too low between meals and that you'll feel faint and weak. But when you're not eating, other hormonal signals trigger your body to release glucose or make more. In one Swedish study by researchers at the Karolinska Institute, students who'd reported that they were sensitive to hypoglycemia (low blood sugar) felt irritable and shaky during a 24-hour fast, but there was actually no difference in their blood sugar levels – it may all have been in their minds.

**Q**      Hang on a minute… My trainer told me that six small meals will fire up my metabolism and stop me feeling peckish. Who's right?

**A**      This is one of those fitness and nutrition "truths" that has been repeated so many times, people are convinced that it's a fact. In one small study at the US National Institute on Aging, researchers found that people who ate only one meal a day did tend to feel hungrier than those who ate three. But beyond eating three meals a day, meal frequency doesn't seem to make a difference to hunger or appetite, so it comes down to what's actually easiest for you. A study published by the International Journal of Obesity showed that people who are overweight tend to snack more often.

The truth is, you will feel hungry when fasting – there's no getting away from that – but rather than a constant unsatisfied feeling, your hunger will come in waves. You'll start to recognize the difference between physical and psychological hunger. And you'll get to eat meals that are big enough to leave you feeling genuinely satisfied when you do eat.

**Q**     Can fasting change my shape?

**A**     For many women, that last bit of surplus weight is carried around the hips and thighs and it simply won't shift. To solve this problem, I suggest looking to the true body professionals.

According to noted intermittent-fasting expert Martin Berkhan, there's a good reason for this. All the cells in our body have "holes" in them known as receptors. To switch activity on and off in those cells, hormones or enzymes enter the receptors. Fat cells contain two types of receptor – beta 2 receptors, which are good at triggering fat burning, and alpha 2 receptors, which aren't. Guess which is mostly found in the fat stores of your lower body? Yes, our hips and thighs have nine times more alpha 2 receptors than beta.

Fasting is the only thing that alters alpha 2 receptor expression in adults – when we're fasting, the alpha 2 receptors are more likely to stay hidden. If you combine this with the fact that GH and catecholamines (hormones released by the adrenal glands) are particularly good at encouraging fat loss, then fasting is a way for your body to release the stubborn fat it retained while you were on traditional diets.

**Q**     What about belly fat?

**A**     All over the Internet you'll see promises that you can get rid of belly fat in a matter of days by taking supplements. We all know that this is simply not true.

Stubborn fat around the middle is linked to a number of factors – including stress, alcohol, lack of exercise and a diet high in refined carbohydrates.

Stress + refined carbohydrates + alcohol = a recipe for belly fat, especially if you're unlucky enough to be genetically predisposed to weight gain around the middle.

**Q**     How does fasting help torch belly fat?

**A**     To burn belly fat, free fatty acids must first be released from your fat cells (this is called lipolysis) and moved into your bloodstream, then transferred into the mitochondria of muscle or organ cells, to be burned (a process known as beta-oxidation).

Glucagon (another pancreatic hormone that has pretty much an equal and opposite effect to insulin) rises around four to five hours after eating, once all the digested nutrients from your last meal have been stored or used up. The purpose of glucagon is to maintain a steady supply of glucose to the brain and red blood cells, which it achieves by breaking down stored carbohydrates and leftover protein fragments in the liver. It also activates hormone-sensitive lipase, which triggers the release of fat from the fat cells, allowing other cells to be fueled by fat as opposed to glucose.

**Q**      What else can I do to help get rid of belly fat?

**A**      Endurance exercise selectively reduces abdominal fat and aids maintenance of lean body mass, so it's great to do in combination with intermittent fasting. Choose a fasting method that will enable you to take regular exercise – gentle activity such as walking will help, but high-intensity training is even better.

Also, a very small recent study, carried out at the University of Oklahoma in the USA, found that quality protein intake was inversely associated with belly fat, so make sure you fuel up on lean proteins (which your fasting plans are rich in), when you are eating.

**Q**      What about losing that last 4.5kg (10lb)?

**A**      This is often the hardest weight to shift. Not only that, it tends to creep back over a matter of weeks after you've finally reached your target weight. A familiar story is the strict diet we follow to get into beach-body shape in time for a holiday: in all the years I've helped people to lose weight, I've lost count of the number of times I've heard people telling me that all their hard work was undone by two weeks of sun, sea and sangria!

Remember that losing weight is all about creating a calorie deficit. Here, fasting is acting in two different ways. First, fasting helps maintain calorie burn – so in theory you can eat more overall and still lose weight. Second, fasting might just be easier to stick to than a boring calorie-counting diet. And when it comes to beach bodies, remember that old saying "a change is as good as a rest". If you're bored of the approach you've taken to weight loss up to now, a short blast of fasting can help you achieve your goal weight without damaging your metabolism.

This is backed up by research. Most of the studies on intermittent fasting show that it can be just as effective for fat loss as traditional diets, but the studies are all designed differently so it's difficult to say exactly which fasting approach will be the most effective for you. Scientific studies on intermittent fasting have shown varying results – from an average weight loss of a few kilos in the first few days, to 8 percent of body weight within eight weeks.

During the first few days of the fast you'll generally lose weight quickly, which can feel very motivating, especially if the scales have been stuck for a while.

One thing to note is that your weight will fluctuate. At first, you'll lose water (because stored glucose holds roughly four times its weight in water, and is quickly used up during a fast), and yesterday's food should make its way through your digestive tract. Alongside this, you'll lose some body fat. But the next day, you'll gain weight via the new intake of water and food. Don't worry! Over time, your average weight will fall. That's why it's important to limit weighing yourself to once or twice a week, and to be consistent in the time and day you use the scales.

# Part 2

# Practice (Unlock Your Metabolism)

# EAT, FAST AND LIVE LONGER

## THE HEALING POWER OF FASTING

Over the last decade I've seen my clients achieve amazing results with fasting. Getting to the optimum weight for your body frame is as much about health as it is about looking and feeling good. Fasting improves health alongside helping to shift the pounds and, just as importantly, it can help heal somebody's relationship with food, which is often at the heart of the struggle with weight.

I firmly believe that what I can achieve with a client during a week of fasting would take me months or possibly years with a conventional nutrition approach. In fact, I'll stick my neck out and say that fasting can and will change how we as a society view healing – if someone told you there was a pill that could reduce the risk of diabetes, cancer and heart disease and keep you looking and feeling young, you'd be tempted to take it, wouldn't you?

Unlike medication, so long as you're sensible about it, there are no harmful side-effects of fasting. Contrast this with the side-effects of common prescription and over-the-counter drugs – even if the chance of side-effects is small, the risks are still real. One study published by the peer-reviewed British Medical Journal into the side-effects of statins (cholesterol-lowering drugs), confirmed cases of increased risk of muscle weakness, cataracts, acute kidney failure, and moderate or severe liver dysfunction. Of course, if disease has taken hold, the benefits of medication will often outweigh the risks. However, we need to be working toward a model of preventative action.

## HOW FASTING PROMOTES HEALING

Nothing in the body, or mind, works in isolation, so it shouldn't come as a surprise to learn that fasting creates a healthy "ripple effect" of sorts.

The over-arching theory is that fasting helps to de-stress the body. When you fast, you give your body a break and a chance to catch up on its inner "to-do" list. We all know how good it feels to have a well-earned holiday and return rested, rejuvenated and with renewed joie de vivre. Well, fasting has a similar effect on your body.

Around 70 percent of your daily energy is spent maintaining internal functions, such as digestion and detoxification. If you're a busy, on-the-go person and don't give your body the best conditions to rest, digest and ultimately heal, ill-health will catch up with you sooner or later.

Have you ever had that sluggish feeling, much like a slow hangover that's really difficult to shake off? Just as your home or office can become dusty and dirty, so your body can become clogged up with toxins and waste matter from the environment around you (more about this later in the chapter). When your body is clean and strong, it's able to eliminate toxins efficiently, but when it becomes overloaded it can become sluggish, overweight (or underweight in some instances) and more susceptible to disease. The result is that "toxic signals", such as aches and pains, irritable bowel, skin complaints, mood swings and fatigue, start to kick in. If these signals are ignored, they allow longer-term chronic health problems to take hold.

Cue fasting. Thousands of studies or observations of both man and animals have established the fact that when the body goes without food, the tissues are called upon in an inverse order of their importance to the organism. What this means is that when you fast, fat is the first tissue to go. And, contrary to expectations, instead of food deprivation causing a debilitating loss of nutrients, in short-term fasts the body retains the majority of these.

Fasting is now considered an acceptable treatment or approach for promoting longevity, improving insulin response, reducing inflammation, boosting cardiovascular health and even for supporting cancer treatment. Fasting may deliver health benefits and more, without many of the unpleasant side-effects produced by other treatments, and, again, without an extortionate price tag.

# FASTING AND ANTI-AGEING

Ageing is inevitable. Everything that keeps us alive from one day to the next can be called your metabolism, and running your body has side-effects. Those side- effects accumulate and eventually will cause problems. Welcome to the reality of ageing… But reality is ever changing and there's good reason to be optimistic. Like looking for the proverbial pot of gold, we seekers of health are all out there, trying to find the elixir of youth.

You're as young or as old as your smallest vital links – your cells. Ageing begins when your normal process of cell regeneration and rebuilding slows down. At a cellular level, the hormone insulin-like growth factor (IGF-1) has both positive and negative effects. Like insulin, it's anabolic, meaning that, in effect, it tells our cells to grow and multiply. If IGF-1 is kept high, our cells constantly divide and multiply, which is good if we're trying to build big muscles and not so good if those cells become damaged and cancerous. High levels of IGF-1 have been linked to prostate cancer and post-menopausal breast cancer. When IGF-1 levels drop, the body slows production of new cells and starts repairing old ones, and DNA damage is more likely to be permanent.

## KEEPING THE HEART AND CIRCULATION HEALTHY

Inflammation is involved in cardiovascular disease, in concert with high levels of "bad" fats in the blood. Most studies on fasting show that it reduces triglyceride levels and improves the ratio of triglycerides to "good" cholesterol (that is, high-density lipoprotein [HDL] – the transport protein that helps remove excess cholesterol from the bloodstream). In animal studies, resistance to what is known as "ischemic injury" – the type of artery damage that's associated with the build-up of plaques and hardening of the arteries – has been seen.

All in all, although the findings are far from clear and lots more research is needed, fasting seems to give the body an internal tune-up and to increase resistance to age-related illnesses.

Going back to those scary statistics from the beginning of this chapter – cardiovascular disease is the leading cause of death worldwide and something that affects us all. In Britain, NHS statistics show that in England in 2007, people aged over 60 were prescribed an average of 42.4 prescription items each. Each time you receive a prescription for an individual drug from your doctor, it counts as one prescription item. That's a whole lot of drugs! Unsurprisingly, medication that treats cardiovascular disease and its risk factors is the most commonly prescribed. I often meet people who want to change their eating habits, not just because they'd like to look and feel better, but because they're shocked by the amount of medication that their own parents are on. As fasting becomes more popular, people are becoming attracted to it as a lifestyle choice that might help their heart and circulatory system stay healthy for longer.

## FASTING AND CANCER

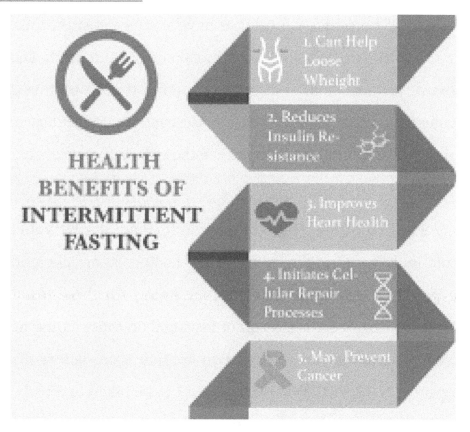

Fasting is considered to be an alternative or complementary treatment for cancer in certain sectors of complementary medicine, and has been popularized by a naturopathic doctor called Max Gerson. However, my focus is not on fasting as a stand-alone treatment but rather on exciting evidence about fasting in cancer prevention and the encouraging results from trials involving fasting during cancer treatment, particularly chemotherapy.

There's evidence that intermittent fasting, and calorie restriction more generally, fights the growth and spread of cancer cells in animals. Often when we read about research on animals, it seems so compelling that we want to see if the same thing will work for us. However, research is so much less likely to be done on humans as, rightly or wrongly, ethics committees are often reluctant to approve the same types of study that are done on animals. As discussed above, in experiments on laboratory animals, diets with 25 percent fewer calories have shown a positive link with longer, healthier life spans. So far there's little empirical study evidence to show the same effect in humans, yet anecdotal evidence is growing that restricting calories, and fasting, activates cell-protecting mechanisms. Research is also underway to find out whether alternate-day fasting can help reduce the risk of breast cancer.

In studies on mice with cancer, fasting appears to improve survival rates after chemotherapy. Hearing of the effects of these animal studies by Valter Longo, ten cancer patients took it upon themselves to try fasting before chemotherapy. The results were published in the medical journal Aging. Of these ten, the majority experienced fewer side-effects as a result of fasting than those eating normally, and the authors concluded that fasting for two to five days before chemotherapy treatment appeared to be safe. This work has yet to be taken to a truly meaningful empirical testing on humans, but it's understandable that cancer patients are excited by the potential of calorie restriction and fasting, not least by it helping the body to mitigate the effects of cancer treatment and specifically chemotherapy.

# DETOXING

Personally, I no longer like the word "detox". It's been used and abused by marketeers in their quest to sell, sell, sell fancy products, when, in fact, detoxing is something that the body does naturally every hour of the day. However, until someone comes up with a better word, "detox" will have to do.

## HOW WE BECOME TOXIC

A toxin is anything that has a detrimental effect on cell function or structure. Toxins are materials that our bodies cannot process efficiently. Over time they build up and, as a result, our systems function below par, leaving us drained, tired and frequently ill. People become "toxic" in many ways – through diet, lifestyle and the environment, as a natural by-product of metabolism, and through genetic lineage. Stress and harmful emotions can also create a kind of toxic environment.

Toxins include, but are not limited to:

- Food additives, flavorings and colorings.

- Household and personal cleaning chemicals, which are both inhaled and absorbed via the skin.

- Agricultural chemicals, such as pesticides, fungicides and herbicides.

- Heavy metals, which occur naturally but are poisonous.

• Oestrogens, which enter the environment due to human usage of the contraceptive pill and HRT.

• Xeno-oestrogens, which are chemicals that mimic oestrogen.

…And here are the most common ways people become toxic on the inside:

• Eating a poor diet. This includes low-fiber foods, fried foods and foods tainted with synthetic chemicals. Unlike live foods (fresh fruits and vegetables), these lack the enzymes that assist proper digestion and assimilation, and the fiber or bulk that assists proper elimination. They're also void of essential vitamins, minerals and other basic nutrients.

• Eating too much. Over-eating puts a great amount of stress on our digestive system. The body must produce hydrochloric acid, pancreatic enzymes, bile and other digestive factors to process a meal. When we over-eat, the digestive system finds it hard to meet the demands placed upon it. The stomach bloats as the digestive system goes into turmoil. Foods aren't broken down properly and tend to lodge in the lower intestine. Vital nutrients are then not absorbed.

• Inadequate water intake. When the body isn't receiving enough water, toxins tend to stagnate, hindering all digestive and eliminative processes.

• Exposure to synthetic chemicals in food and environmental pollutants. A clean, strong system can metabolize and excrete many pollutants, but when the body is weak or constipated, they're stored as unusable substances. As more and different chemicals enter the body, they tend to interact with those already there, forming second-generation chemicals that can be far more harmful than the originals.

• Being stressed. Stress hinders proper digestion, absorption and elimination of foods.

• Overuse of antibiotics. Antibiotics have a damaging effect on the intestines, especially if they're taken for extensive periods of time. Reducing the use of unnecessary antibiotics will also help minimize the very real danger of bacterial resistance.

• Lack of exercise. This lowers metabolic efficiency, and without circulatory stimulation, the body's natural cleansing systems are weakened.

• Eating late at night. The human body uses sleep to repair, rebuild and restore itself. In essence, the body uses the sleeping hours to cleanse and build. When a person goes to sleep with a full stomach, the body isn't at rest but is busy digesting and processing food. In addition, the body requires gravity to assist the passage of food from the stomach down the digestive tract.

**Q**      If the body detoxes itself anyway, why bother to do anything further?

**A**      Just as your home or office can become dusty and dirty, so your body can become clogged up with toxins and waste matter from the environment. A healthy body is able to disarm toxins by breaking them down, storing them in fat tissue or excreting them. However, here's the crux – many, if not most,

people are depleted in the nutrients needed to detox optimally, and chronic health problems, sluggishness and weight gain are common results.

If you've never given your digestion much thought, don't beat yourself up about being neglectful. Unlike the head or the tips of the fingers, the gut contains very few nerve endings. What this means is, we're not so aware when things aren't working well. When you have a headache, you feel every throbbing pulse and do something about it. In contrast, gut problems go unresolved and uncared for over long periods.

The good news is, when you improve digestion, a whole range of seemingly unrelated health issues can improve. For example, it's not only the job of the white blood cells (the leukocytes) to defend your body since the digestive system forms the basis of your immune system with the action of beneficial bacteria. Improving the ecology of the gut can be achieved with a juice fast and healthy diet.

## USING A JUICE FAST TO DETOX

A juice fast stands head and shoulders above other fasting techniques in its self-healing effect and is often mentioned in the context of detoxing the body.

Juice fasting is based on consuming juices and broths only, whereas intermittent fasting adds lean protein and fat for the feeling of fullness. Studies have shown that eating as little as 10g (¼oz) of essential amino acids (found in high-quality proteins) can switch off autophagy. Therefore, a juice fast is best placed to give your body a good "spring clean" because juices are typically very low in protein.

The simple act of juicing a fruit or vegetable will help you absorb more of the nutrients from it. The caveat here is that you should make the juice fresh rather than drink pasteurized fruit juice from a carton or bottle. The process of juicing eliminates a lot of the fiber that needs to be digested. Cutting out the bulk and drinking only the juice means that you can very effectively hit your antioxidant targets in one small cup. Juice provides tiny "particles" of nutrients that are readily absorbed into the bloodstream.

Fresh juices provide a highly effective fast-track and – importantly – easy delivery mechanism for the body to absorb and process key vitamins, minerals and plant chemicals (phytonutrients) that are so beneficial to our health. A fresh juice contains a concentration of nutrients that have been separated from pulp, making it easier to consume what's required to assist the healing process. In essence, a fresh juice should be considered more of a body tonic than a tasty drink.

**Q**      Will I get withdrawal symptoms on a juice fast?

**A**      The folklore of fasting is littered with stories about the dramatic side-effects of a juice fast. This is usually because the contrast between the diet and lifestyle before and after is simply too great. Or, in some cases, the enterprising individual has decided to "retox", that is go on an almighty bender before entering detox – not a good idea.

One of the most dramatic side-effects I ever witnessed was when a client was coming off a 20-year-long diet cola habit during a juice-fasting retreat. Her symptoms were akin to what you'd expect from coming off a class-A drug. The rest of the detox group watched mesmerized at her descent from bubbly, bouncy guest on arrival to a sweating, vomiting, pale-faced shadow of her former self after just 24 hours of juicing. Even I was a little worried. Luckily, her troubled time was followed by a rapid and dramatic improvement two days later, at which point she declared that she felt "reborn" and would never touch a drop of cola again.

So, learn from my diet cola story and start with a transition diet. Fasting can be a challenge physically and psychologically. I recommend having at least three days on the Countdown Plan to prepare. Juice fasting should be undertaken for between one and five days for optimum results – usually once or twice a year. Any longer requires more management and should only be considered when there are adequate reserves (body fat) or if there's a specific medical condition. Some people find that weekend-long juice fasts four times a year are helpful.

**Q**      What are the most common side-effects of a juice fast?

**A**      Let me be frank – a juice fast isn't a good idea for a romantic break or naughty weekend away. During a juice fast the capacity of the eliminative organs – lungs, liver, kidneys, and skin – is greatly increased, and masses of accumulated metabolic wastes and toxins are quickly expelled. It's like pressing the accelerator button on your body's waste disposal unit. As part of the eliminative process, your body will be cleansing itself of old, accumulated wastes and toxins. This typically throws up symptoms such as offensive breath, dark urine, increased faecal waste, skin eruptions, perspiration and increased mucus. As I said, it's not exactly romantic!

Your digestive system is the star of a fasting program. Poor digestion can be a hidden cause of weight gain, or more accurately, water retention. For example, if your body's responding to an allergy or intolerance, it will often retain water. So, when fasting, there's often a "quick-win" water loss that equates to an extra kilo being lost.

**Q**     What about fiber?

**A**     The process of juicing extracts the pulp (fiber) of the fruits and vegetables so on a juice fast it's a good idea to restore some bulk to maintain a healthy transit of waste matter through the gastrointestinal tract. Psyllium husks, a soluble form of fiber, do just the trick as, when taken with adequate amounts of fluids, they absorb water to form a large mass. In people with constipation, this mass stimulates the bowel to move, whereas in people with diarrhea it can slow things down and reduce bowel movements.

Some recent research also shows that psyllium husks may lower cholesterol. It's thought that the fiber stimulates the conversion of cholesterol into bile acid and increases bile acid excretion. In addition, psyllium husks may even decrease the intestinal absorption of cholesterol.

Psyllium comes from the plant Plantago ovata and is native to India. It is readily available in health food shops and online stores, either as husks or in powdered form. In non-fasting, normal dietary conditions, whole grains provide dietary fiber and similar beneficial effects to psyllium, so a supplement isn't needed unless recommended by your health care practitioner.

**Q**     Can colon cleansing help?

**A**     Your bowels are not just "poo pipes". Toxins and metabolic wastes from the blood and tissues are discharged into the intestinal canal to be excreted from the body. Not surprisingly, one of the long-established techniques to support the body's elimination organs during a fast is colon hydrotherapy or enemas. This is a technique that involves taking in water into the large intestine, also known as the bowel, to assist the removal of waste.

# Part 3

# Results (Rejuvenate)

# EAT, FAST AND PERFORM BETTER

## CAN FASTING GIVE YOU A YOUNGER BRAIN?

The potential benefits of fasting go beyond weight loss and physical health. If you've ever found yourself befuddled about where you could possibly have left your keys/phone/purse/marbles, you'll know that memory loss is a very frightening thing. The threat of long-term conditions like Alzheimer's is arguably one of the most worrying aspects of ageing. But there is hope. Researchers at the National Institute on Aging in Baltimore have found evidence that fasting for one or two days each week may help protect the brain against Alzheimer's, Parkinson's and other brain diseases.

## ISN'T BREAKFAST IMPORTANT "BRAIN FOOD"?

Children who eat breakfast tend to perform better in cognitive tests, but this doesn't seem to be the case for adults. Studies have shown that short-term food reduction doesn't actually impair cognitive function in adults. Prolonged dieting, on the other hand, does. This means that the perceived deterioration in brain function may, in fact, have a psychological cause – rather than being caused by a dip in blood sugar, lack of concentration may be a result of the stress of being "on a diet" (the way it tends to make you feel grumpy, miserable, and obsessive about food). Of course, it's true that the brain uses glucose for fuel, but as we've seen in previous chapters, our bodies have enough stored glucose to see us through a short fast.

In one study, published in the American Journal of Clinical Nutrition, scientists observed that fasting and non-fasting groups of adults performed similarly in cognitive tests, even after two days without food. This is thought to relate to adaptive mechanisms – as adults, when we don't have food available, it's important that we have the mental clarity to go out and find it. Our hunter- gatherer ancestors didn't have the option to pop out to the supermarket to grab a snack, and those who could think more clearly when hungry were more likely to be able to find food or outsmart predators. This was a survival advantage, and so the genetic factors that maintained cognitive function when food was scarce were passed on. As there haven't been dramatic changes in our genes since caveman times, it makes sense that the ability to think clearly when we haven't eaten for a while should still be the norm.

## FASTING AND BRAIN HEALTH

Professor Mark Mattson, a renowned researcher at the National Institute on Aging, has dedicated his career to studying the effects of fasting on brain ageing. Until now, all his research has been on mice, but there's now enough evidence of the beneficial effects of fasting on the brains of mice to begin research on humans.

At the National Institute on Aging, mice have been bred to develop a susceptibility to Alzheimer's disease. If they are then put on a "fast food" diet which is high in sugar, they experience an earlier onset of learning and memory problems. But if they're made to fast every other day, they find it much easier to remember their way around a maze. Brain scans on the mice show that fasting actually encourages new brain cells (neurons) to form by placing a mild level of stress on the brain cells, which encourages them to build up a resistance to future stress, as well as building new proteins. Other researchers have found that fasting also increases the rate of autophagy in the brain, thereby getting rid of any damaged "grey matter" and making way for healthy new cells. So, while it's too early to tell whether fasting is the miracle cure for memory loss and age- related brain diseases, the research definitely sounds promising.

## WHAT ELSE CAN I DO TO KEEP MY BRAIN YOUNG?

Sadly, the exact reasons why some people are susceptible to diseases such as Alzheimer's are unclear. It's generally accepted that diets rich in fruit, vegetables and healthy fats from fish, avocados and olives (typically like the Mediterranean diet) are associated with good brain health. What's good for the body is also good for the brain!

One of the most important things that you can do for your body and brain is to get active and regular fasting might just help you do that. Recent studies published in the Archives of Internal Medicine indicate that the more active we are as we get older – even if it's just gentle walking – the longer our brains will stay healthy. It sounds like the recipe for a healthy brain could be fasting combined with an active lifestyle and a real-food based diet – just what I have in mind!

## CAN FASTING MAKE YOU FASTER?

I have to declare an interest here... For a few years I've loved the release that running has given me, especially after having my second baby. In fact, I've been a competitive soul from day dot. In my early youth I was good at badminton and represented Scotland in the game. In those days, not much attention was paid to sports nutrition, and since badminton is a largely anaerobic discipline it was possible to get by without thinking too much about what you were eating. Now, of course, everything has changed. Nutritionists feature large in all serious sport - not least, I imagine, because the "quick fix" route of banned substances has come under the spotlight, and, of course, we're all more aware of nutrition's role in exercise.

My running has become something of a "fix" – a means of releasing tension, either before the stress of the school run, or after the stress of a day's work. My usual preparation used to consist of an espresso and a mostly empty stomach. While that works for a quick half-hour run, it was only when I stepped up to training for the London Marathon in 2011 that I became more scientific and observant of my nutritional requirements. I also wondered whether fasting during training or pre-event could make a person run faster.

## COMMON QUESTIONS AND ANSWERS

**Q**     What's the truth about sports drinks?

**A**     If you're a keen runner or cyclist, or harbor ambitions to run a marathon, you're probably aware of the importance of getting plenty of carbs. It's impossible to open up a running magazine or take part in a race without being bombarded with adverts for the latest energy drink or gel.

It's a fact that topping up your fuel levels with sugar – whether from fruit juice, sweets or expensive sports drinks – can make you run faster if your existing energy levels are low. Countless sports nutrition studies confirm that they do benefit performance. And the British public are buying into the dream en masse. In 2010, we drank 600 million liters of energy drinks and sports drinks.

However, topping up your blood sugar during exercise is only beneficial if you're taking part in high-intensity exercise that lasts for more than an hour, such as running a half-marathon or competing in a football match. In other cases, it won't do you any favors at all.

**Q**     What about fasting and exercise during Ramadan?

**A**     Interest in the effects of fasting on fitness has increased in recent years, inspired by studies on what happens to Muslim athletes during the month of Ramadan. During Ramadan, Muslims are required to observe a period of fasting from dawn until sunset. This includes avoiding not only food, but fluids too. As the dates of Ramadan change from year to year, this means that it can take place across major events in the sporting calendar, such as the 2012 Olympics. If you believe the sports nutrition adverts, you may think that not being able to eat or drink regularly would ruin an athlete's chances of winning, but that doesn't necessarily seem to be the case.

While most medal contenders at the 2012 Olympics seem to have taken the opportunity to postpone their fast until later in the year, in 1980 Tanzanian runner Suleiman Nyambui won silver in the 5,000 meters while observing the Ramadan fast. The effects of fasting on athletes' ability to compete and train during Ramadan are mixed. Several studies summarizing the research were published in the Journal of Sports Science in 2012. The overall picture was that the effects of fasting on performance are minimal, so long as overall nutritional intake and other factors, such as quality of sleep, are maintained.

Nevertheless, training while fasting – especially in the case of Ramadan, where athletes are also likely to be dehydrated through avoiding water – may make you feel more tired or reduce the amount of effort that you're able to put in. But, for mere mortals rather than Olympians, intermittent fasting has the promising ability to improve overall fitness or sports performance.

**Q**     Should I cut carbs?

**A**     As mentioned at the beginning of this chapter, the roots of how fasting may benefit performance are in our evolutionary past. Our caveman ancestors simply didn't have the opportunity to fuel up with carbohydrates before they went off to forage and hunt. Cycles of feast and famine meant that the ability to perform extended periods of physical activity on an empty stomach was an advantage when it came to survival. It's thought that our genetic make-up hasn't changed much in the 10,000 or so years since. So, it makes sense, in theory, that humans are designed to exercise without taking on extra fuel. At all times, our bodies burn both fat and carbohydrate for energy. While our storage capacity for carbohydrate is limited to around 500 calories-worth, most of us have more than enough fat stores to keep us going for a while. Say you're 70kg (11st) and your body fat is 25 percent – that means you have over 150,000 calories of fat in storage.

Aerobic training increases the proportion of fat to carbohydrate burned, making it easier to exercise for long periods of time. Just as the body adapts to any training stimulus by getting stronger or fitter, the idea is that training when fasting – when stored carbohydrate levels are low – stimulates the body to become even more efficient at using stored fat for fuel. While it might therefore seem like a no-brainer that exercising without extra carbohydrate will help your body adapt, it has long been recommended that endurance athletes consume a carbohydrate-rich diet.

Carbohydrate is stored in muscles as glycogen, where it can easily be broken down into glucose to fuel movement. Most research continues to emphasize the importance of adequate carbohydrate intake, before, during and after exercise. This is particularly important during high- intensity events, where glucose is the main fuel – stored fat is pretty good at fueling slow and steady movement, but it's glucose that your body turns to when you want to move fast. In events or training that last over an hour, it's generally recommended that 30–60g (1–2¼oz) of carbohydrate is consumed per hour, in the form of drinks, gels or food.

The mistake that many of us make is to rely on topping up our carbohydrate stores too much. This could also be the reason why many people don't lose weight when they start exercising. A typical bottle of sports drink can take half an hour of leisurely cycling to burn off, so if that's all you manage, and you add in a post-workout snack too, you could even find yourself gaining weight!

**Q** What happens when you train while fasting?

**A** Looking back to a study carried out by the US Army in 1988, there's no need to fear running out of glucose if you haven't eaten for a day. In fact, it seems to be possible to exercise for just as long after a three-and-a-half day- fast as it is after an overnight fast when working at a low intensity. Researchers in the same study found that blood glucose levels were maintained too.

In another small study published in the Journal of Physical Activity and Health, this time on healthy people who exercised at a relatively high intensity for an hour-and-a-half, fasting for 16–18 hours didn't impede their efforts. Interestingly, drinking a sports drink didn't make them feel or perform better either.

Meanwhile, researchers at Pennington Biomedical Research Center have discovered that consuming carbohydrates during exercise can actually decrease the expression of genes that are involved in fat metabolism. So, the more carbs you take in during exercise, the worse your body gets at tapping into its fat stores!

Sticking to plain water, or a calorie-free drink, increases the proportion of fat burned during exercise because less glucose is available. When you consume a sports drink, the glucose is rapidly delivered to your blood and provides an instant source of fuel. Without this, you need to tap into your body's fat stores.

**Q**     What's meant by "train low, race high"?

**A**     "Train low" means that some training is done without carbs to encourage the body to burn fat. As the bulk of modern sports nutrition research highlights the role of carbohydrates in enhancing performance under race conditions, the "race high" part involves taking on standard sports drinks or gels during events.

"Train low" training is different from simply training after an overnight fast, when muscle glycogen levels are still relatively high. Studies investigating the "train low" approach deplete participants' glycogen stores by putting them through an hour or more of aerobic training. After an hour's rest, participants then complete up to an hour of high-intensity exercise, all with only water to drink.

But be careful because training in a glycogen-depleted state has its risks.

These include increased levels of stress hormones, muscle breakdown, fatigue and lowered immune response. If, while fasting, you decide to add some endurance training to your schedule, especially at a high intensity, it's probably best, initially, to limit it to once a week. Allow plenty of time for recovery, and monitor your response, stopping if you feel unwell or fatigued.

## FASTING FOR A STRONGER BODY

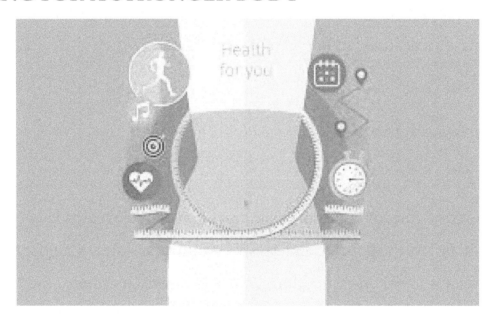

Weight-training enthusiasts use intermittent fasting as a technique to build lean mass and lose fat, with the goal of achieving a "shredded" or "ripped" physique. The explosion in popularity of intermittent fasting over the past few years is in part due to fitness experts such as Martin Berkhan, who designed the "Lean Gains" 16/8 hour fast. This method focuses the fast around the times you're scheduled to work out. The reason for this is that, in order to build muscle, you need to be in positive energy and protein balance after your workout, otherwise your muscles will be consumed for energy instead of getting bigger. Therefore, while the workout is done in the fasted state, the biggest meal of the day is right after the workout. Some people also take "branched-chain amino acid" supplements to maximize levels of growth hormone and to kick-start the muscle- building process.

## FASTING AND MOTIVATION

The final motivator, when thinking about incorporating fasting with exercise, is that it could give you more energy to train. There are lots of arguments over whether diet or exercise is more important when it comes to losing weight.

You may be familiar with the saying "you can't out-train a bad diet". While it's probably true that exercise alone isn't going to get you the body you want if you pay no attention to what you eat, dieting without exercise isn't a good idea either. After all, exercise comes with an impressive array of health benefits itself from heart and lung health, to stress relief, to maintaining strong bones.

When it comes to muscle strength and the way you look, exercise is the clear winner over diet. Researchers at Ann Arbor University in Michigan looked at how women's bodies responded to diet alone versus exercise alone. They found that, as expected, diet was more effective at reducing body weight, but exercise was more effective when it came to losing fat and maintaining muscle.

The thing is, getting the motivation to exercise can be hard when you're "on a diet" because you're always eating less than you're burning off and you often feel like you just don't have the energy. The good thing about fasting is that the gaps between meals are longer so when you do eat, you get to eat more. This means that you can time your exercise around the times when you've eaten and are feeling energetic. You're more likely to work harder!

# MEDITATION

For those with ambition above and beyond the physical benefits of fasting, getting into the fasting state of mind can be helped by meditation, and if you have the time and inclination at least once in your life, a week's retreat can take the fasting experience to another level.

Meditation can be viewed in scientific terms for its effects on the mind and the body. During meditation, a marked increase in blood flow slows heart rate, and high blood pressure drops to within normal ranges. Recent research indicates that meditation can also boost the immune system and reduce free radicals – in effect, a slowing down of the ageing process.

There's much talk about the power of meditation and how you can use your mind to manifest great piles of money. But, becoming more aware of your mind is not just about manipulating it or attempting only to have positive thoughts – rather, it's about the ability to direct your attention toward or away from the mind at will.

My most intensive fast was on a 10-day silent meditation retreat during my time in India. One evening, five days into the experience when I was seriously doubting my judgement about freezing my butt off in a cold cave in the Himalayas, I had what I've come to realize was a "breakthrough" moment. In spiritual terms I'd describe it as a moment of grace. With a raw, pure energy of infinite magnitude, my mind flashed through formative experiences – good and bad – that had shaped my life. As my mind was swept along on this emotional rollercoaster, my body conveniently left the room, leaving me nowhere to run or hide… or at least that was how it felt!

When I first started to meditate, I tried too hard. Furiously studying the science of the mind or contorting your face into Zen-like expressions won't work. The only way to experience meditation is actually to experience it. It can be maddening. You'll be trying to meditate for hours and then, just when you're ready to give up, you might get a flash of something akin to what you were aiming for. Yet, in that momentary shift you might see how you could choose to do a few things differently, or how some really small things have a huge impact on you, and how easy it would be to make a few minor changes. Many great thinkers have talked about breakthroughs and inspiration. The most famous of all was probably Albert Einstein, who said that no problem can be solved from the same level of consciousness that created it.

So, if you do manage to get your mind to stop its usual chatter through meditation, try asking yourself a question when all is calm. For example, if you always react to something uncomfortable by quashing the emotion with food, then meditation can create a gap to ask why. Sometimes there's a clear answer to that question, and sometimes there isn't. Usually, it takes a bit of time.

## YOGA

Yoga is often lumped together with meditation since the kind of person who likes yoga is often into meditation, and vice versa. For people with a poor attention span, yoga can be a good way of getting into a calm state without the need ever to sit cross-legged.

There are many forms of yoga and it's a case of having a go and seeing which suits you best. Regardless of which tradition you choose, good yoga teachers can make you walk out of the class feeling a foot taller and ready to take on the world. My advice would be:

- If you're gentle by nature, try Hatha.

- If you're into precision and detail, go for Iyengar.

- If you like the spiritual side of yoga, opt for Sivananda.

- If you want yoga to help you sleep, try Yin.

• If you're fit and physical, Ashtanga or Vinyasa "flow" yoga will be more your bag.

• If you really want to sweat, try Bikram, or "hot yoga". It's not for the faint hearted and has some medical contra-indications, but it's considered seriously addictive by devotees.

# ANTI-AGING TIPS FOR FASTING

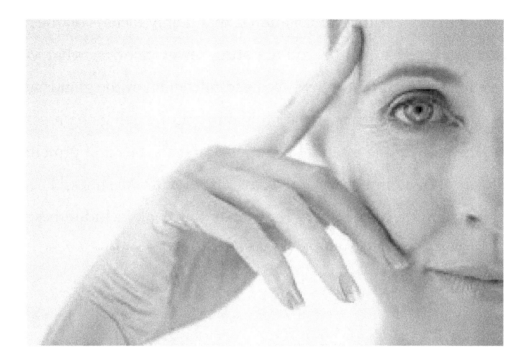

There are far too many tips which would enable you achieve that anti-aging look and feel. However, we are going to be grouping them for you to easily process and remember.

# EAT WELL

The problem with most fasting information is that it only focuses on the fasting bit, not on what you need to eat. If you're eating fewer calories, what you do eat becomes even more important. Why? We need nutrients for the glands and organs of the body to thrive and burn fat. Restricting nutrients by living on processed foods can deprive the body of the essential vitamins, minerals, fats and proteins it needs to maintain a healthy immune system, recover from injury or illness, keep muscles strong and maintain the metabolism. That's why this book includes these nutrition rules and practical fasting plans and recipes to help guide you.

## RULE 1: ONLY EAT "REAL" FOOD

This means no fake food and no diet-drinks. If you grew up in the UK, chances are you'll have fond memories of bright orange corn snacks and fizzy drinks that turned your tongue red or blue. It's to be hoped that now you're "all grown up 'n' stuff", you eat lots of rocket and Parmesan salads, roasted artichoke and monkfish. If only that was the case for all of us. Celebrity chefs may make out that this is the norm but it just isn't. Most people still eat a diet full of processed, refined, low-fiber, nutrient-deficient foods.

Not all processed food is bad, though. In fact, some of it's great. Canned food without added sugar or salt and freshly-frozen fruit and veg are just a couple of examples of stellar staples for your larder. It's the low-calorie, low-fat, oh-so-easy snacks and meals that you need to watch out for since they're often loaded with chemicals and hidden sugars.

Heavily processed foods can also be high in chemicals. There's a real and present danger that chemicals in the environment may have a blocking effect on hormones that control weight loss. When the brain is affected by toxins, it's possible that hormone signaling is impaired. The reason why we're unsure as to the extent of the problem is that it's impossible to test for the thousands of chemicals that are contributing to the "cocktail" effect on the body. Err on the side of caution and control what you can. Keep foods "real"!

But what makes up a real-food diet?

## *PROTEIN*

Protein is made up of amino acids, often called the "building blocks of life", and we need all of them to stay alive and thrive. Proteins from animal sources – meat, dairy, fish and eggs – contain all the amino acids and are therefore classed as "complete" proteins. Soya beans also fall into this category. Once and for all, eggs are healthy. Eggs have had a tough time of it over the years. First the salmonella scare, then the unfair link to cholesterol. Eggs are low in saturated fat and if you eat eggs in the morning, you're less likely to feel hungry later in the day.

Vegetable sources provide incomplete proteins. If you're vegetarian or vegan, you'll get your protein from nuts, seeds, legumes and grains but you need a good variety of these to ensure that you get the full range of essential amino acids.

## TOP TIP:

• Include more beans and lentils in your meals. Examples include kidney beans, butter beans, chickpeas or red and green lentils. They're rich in protein and contain complex carbohydrates, which provide slow and sustained energy release. They also contain fiber, which may help to control your blood fats. Try adding them to stews, casseroles, soups and salads.

## CARBOHYDRATES

Carbs are one of the most controversial topics in nutrition and weight loss. For years we've been told that we eat too much fat, and that saturated fat is the main cause of heart disease. But recently, some experts have challenged this view, suggesting that carbohydrate is responsible for the obesity epidemic and a whole host of diseases. Should we cut carbs, avoid fat or simply reduce our food intake and exercise more?

When the body is starved of carbohydrates it looks for energy in its glycogen stores. Water binds to every gram of glycogen so it's easy to get dramatic weight loss – the only problem is that it's mostly water weight! Along with those glycogen stores you'll begin to lose fat but not at a rate higher than a healthier (and easier) weight-loss method.

The truth is there are healthy fats and healthy carbohydrates. Avoiding carbs altogether is unnecessary and potentially dangerous. The key is in recognizing that not all carbs are created equal. Low glycemic index (GI) carbohydrates, found in fiber-rich fruits, beans, unrefined grains and vegetables, are important for good health and can actively support weight loss – for example, through reducing appetite and energy intake.

However, high-GI refined carbohydrates, such as those found in soft drinks, white bread, pastries, certain breakfast cereals and sweeteners, not only make it harder to lose weight but could damage long-term health. Studies show that eating a lot of high-GI carbohydrates can increase the risk of heart disease and Type-2 diabetes.

There's been a lot of research on low-carbohydrate diets in recent years. It was initially thought that they may damage bone and kidney health, but this doesn't seem to be the case unless you have a pre-existing kidney problem. Lowcarb diets can be effective for weight loss and also improve risk factors for heart disease and diabetes. However, they do carry risks.

First, the low intake of fruit, vegetables and whole grains on a lowcarb diet reduces the intake of certain vitamins and minerals, notably folate, which is vital for women who may become pregnant. Second, cutting out unrefined carbohydrates dramatically reduces the amount of fiber in the diet, which leads to constipation and changes the balance of gut bacteria. In the long term, this may increase the risk of colorectal cancer. Finally, eating a lowcarb diet based on animal protein has been associated with a significantly higher risk of mortality. High levels of meat and dairy create substances called prostaglandins, which are inflammatory. Inflammation is bad news for the body. Side-effects of a very lowcarb diet can include bad breath, hair loss, mood swings, constipation and fatigue. In my opinion, this is too high a price to pay when weight loss can be achieved just as quickly without the side-effects.

For this reason, while I'd never recommend cutting out carbohydrates as a food group, my recipes focus on unrefined, low-GI carbs from whole foods rather than refined, high-GI carbs. As well as improving health, low-GI carbs release glucose into the bloodstream more slowly, which leads to a more sustained energy release, rather than the peaks and crashes you tend to experience if you eat a lot of high-GI carbs.

## TOP TIP:

•      Eat bulky carbs to become slim. When you choose "big" foods like fruits, vegetables, salads and soups, which are bulked up by fiber and water, you're eating a lot of food that fills you up, but not a lot of calories.

## FAT

Since fat is the greatest source of calories, eating less of it can help you to lose weight. However, fat is actually a vital nutrient and is an important part of your diet because it supplies the essential fatty acids needed for vitamin absorption, healthy skin, growth and the regulation of bodily functions. In fact, eating too little fat can actually cause a number of health problems.

The right kinds of fat, in the right amounts, can also help you to feel fuller for longer, so try not to think of fat as your mortal diet enemy, but rather a useful ally in the pursuit of your healthier lifestyle! Adding a little fat to your meals helps your body absorb nutrients and enhances the flavor of your food, so recipes have been created with this in mind. Choose monounsaturated fats or oils (e.g., olive oil and rapeseed oil) as these types of fats are better for your heart. Coconut oil can be a good choice for cooking as it's heat-stable.

## TOP TIPS:

• Increase essential fats – aim for at least two portions of oily fish a week. Examples include mackerel, sardines, salmon and pilchards. Oily fish contains a type of polyunsaturated fat called omega 3, which helps protect against heart disease. If you don't eat fish, use flaxseed oil in salad dressing and snack on walnuts.

• If you use butter, stick to a thin scraping on bread and just a smidgen for flavor in cooking.

• Choose lean meat and fish as low-fat alternatives to fatty meats.

• Choose lower-fat dairy foods such as skimmed or semi-skimmed milk and reduced-fat natural yogurt.

• Grill, poach, steam or oven bake instead of frying or cooking with oil or other fats.

• Watch out for creamy sauces and dressings – swap them for tomato-based sauces. Add herbs, lemon, spices and garlic to reduced-fat meals to boost flavor.

• Use cheese as a topping, not a meal – in other words, no macaroni cheese! Choose cheese with a strong flavor, such as Parmesan or goat's cheese so that you only need to use a small amount.

## RULE 2: CUT OUT SUGAR

Too much sugar makes you fat and has an ageing effect on the skin. Sugar links with collagen and elastin and reduces the elasticity of the skin, making you look older than your years. The recipes I provide use low-sugar fruits to add a little sweetness – and the occasional drizzle of a natural sweetener such as honey is fine – but, in general, sugar is bad news and best avoided.

*TOP TIP:*

• Stick to dark chocolate if you need a chocolate "fix" (which simply is the case sometimes!), as most people need less of it to feel satisfied.

## RULE 3: WATCH THE ALCOHOL

Over the years the alcohol content of most drinks has gone up. A drink can now have more units than you think. A small glass of wine (175ml/5½fl cup) could be as much as two units. Remember, alcohol contains empty calories so think about cutting back further if you're trying to lose weight. That's a maximum of two units of alcohol per day for a woman and three units per day for a man. For example, a single pub measure (25ml/¾fl oz) of spirit is about one unit, and a half pint of lager, ale, bitter or cider is one to one-and-a-half units.

*TOP TIP:*

• If you're out for the evening, try out some healthy soft drinks such as tonic with cordial, or an alcohol-free grape juice as a tasty substitute to wine. Alcohol-free beers are also becoming increasingly popular and are available in most pubs and bars.

## RULE 4: EAT FRUIT, DON'T DRINK IT

If you consume around 1 liter (35fl oz/4 cups) fruit juice, remember you'll be imbibing 500 calories. That's fine if you're juice fasting, but too much if it's simply a snack. You could tuck into a baked potato with tuna and two pieces of fruit for the same number of calories.

## TOP TIPS:

• Choose herbal teas (especially green tea, which may aid fat loss).


• Feel free to have a cup or two of tea or coffee. A small amount of milk is allowed but keep it to a splash when you're fasting.

• Sip water throughout the fast, aiming for a fluid intake of around 1.2–2 liters (40–70fl oz/4¾–8 cups) a day. This will not only help to keep hunger pangs at bay, it will also keep you hydrated.

## RULE 5: AVOID THE PITFALLS

*TOP TIPS:*

• Top up before you fast. When you first start fasting, you may feel hungry during the times when you'd normally have a meal and you may also feel slightly light-headed if you have sugary foods as your last meal. This isn't a sign that you're wasting away or entering starvation mode, and these feelings of hunger will usually subside once that usual meal time has passed. Try to get your carbohydrate intake from fruit, vegetables and whole grains and eat a good amount of protein, which will fill you up for longer. Following the fasting plans will make this as straightforward as possible.

• Stock up for quick meals. Make sure you always have ingredients in your fridge and cupboards for meals that can be put together quickly, such as stir- fries, soups and salads.

• Don't polish off the kids' plates. Eating the children's leftovers is a fast track to weight gain for parents. Put the plates straight into the sink or dishwasher when the children have finished their meal, so you won't be tempted!

• Downsize your dinner plate. Much of our hunger and satiation is psychological. If we see a huge plate only half full, we'll feel like we haven't eaten enough. But if the plate is small but completely filled, we'll subconsciously feel that we have eaten enough.

• Beware of the Frappuccino effect. Black coffee only contains about 10 calories but a milky coffee can contain anything from 100 calories for a standard small cappuccino to a whopping 350+ calories for a Grande with all the trimmings. Much like the plate size, shrink your cup size and shrink your waist line. Don't be afraid to ask for half the milk – spell it out: "Don't fill up the cup." I do it all the time and the best baristas get it right first time!

• The sandwich has become the ubiquitous carb-laden "lunch on the go". Lose the top piece of bread to cut your refined carbohydrates and instead fill up with a small bag of green salad leaves and healthy dressing.

• Don't try to change everything at once. Bad habits are hard enough to break as it is. Focus on breaking one at a time.

• If you're a parent, choose your meal skipping wisely. I've tried fasting with a toddler who doesn't understand why Mummy isn't eating and will, quite literally, shove a fistful of tuna pasta into my mouth.

• Get the portions right. If you're restricting the number of meals you're having, it makes sense that the portion sizes need to be bigger than they would be if you were eating five mini-meals a day. Use the recipe section as a guide to how big your portions should be.

# FASTING SAFELY

By now I hope that you have an open mind to the many benefits of fasting and that you're excited about giving it a go. If you've read this book and are still trying to decide if, when, or how to give fasting a try, remember that you'll only ever truly "get it" by trying it for yourself.

Before you launch headlong into your new fasting lifestyle, here are a few words of caution. Although fasting has been around for millennia, the science on how and when to fast is in its early stages. For example, there's very little research on how fasting affects fertility.

There are some people who should avoid fasting completely, some who should seek medical advice first, and some situations where it might not be right for you. Fasting isn't something that you should just jump into, and it doesn't suit everyone.

## WHEN NOT TO FAST

You should avoid fasting if any of the following apply:

• You are pregnant, breastfeeding, or actively trying for a baby (it's okay to fast if you're getting your body ready to conceive, but please don't consider fasting if there's any chance you could already be pregnant).

• You have ever experienced an eating disorder.

• You are underweight

You should seek medical advice first if any of the following apply:

• You have a long-term medical condition such as cancer, diabetes, ulcerative colitis, epilepsy, anemia, liver, kidney or lung disease.

• You have a condition that affects your immune system.

• You are on medication, particularly medicines that control your blood sugar, blood pressure or blood lipids (cholesterol).

## POSSIBLE SIDE-EFFECTS AND HOW TO MANAGE THEM

As we learnt earlier in the book, fasting may make you feel a bit "yucky" at first. Many juice fasters experience headaches through caffeine withdrawal, and feeling hungry is natural when you first try a fast. These effects don't usually last long, and most people find that they're outweighed by the positive effects of fasting.

More serious side-effects may include:

- Dehydration or over-hydration.

- Feeling dizzy or light-headed.

- Extreme fatigue.

- Constipation.

- Nausea or vomiting.

- Insomnia.

- Irregular periods.

Always err on the side of caution and stop the fast if you don't feel well. You can minimize the risk of some side-effects by approaching the fast safely.

# CONCLUSION

If you've read this book and are still trying to decide if, when or how to give fasting a try, stop! Don't intellectualize or rationalize it. You'll only ever truly "get it" by trying for yourself.

It is a leap of faith to believe that something as simple as drinking juice can do what pills and potions cannot. So, you just need to make the leap and see what happens.

You need to remember that healing from the inside is something your body is designed to do. If you create the right conditions, the body will respond. Fasting can create the right internal environment for healing and positive change to occur.

The same process happens emotionally, too. There is nothing quite like the perspective or creative leap that occurs in the mind when you take time out from your norm. Just imagine what life could be like if you followed your dreams.

I know because that is exactly what happened to me. Before I end this book, I want to tell you the story of the TV series that first spread the word of the power of fasting. It's something I am asked about all the time, all over the world, and it's a story I've never told fully before now.

I admitted at the beginning of the book that I kind of stumbled upon fasting. I had already studied Nutritional Medicine so I had a good grounding in the science of sound eating. However, when I started using juice fasting, first on my own and then with clients, the results were so astonishing that it was the push I needed to give up a six-figure salary, sell a house and drive to Spain with nothing more than the notion of following my dream to set up my first juice- fasting retreat.

One year later I had learned the local lingo, made lifelong friends and was enjoying a wonderful lifestyle of yoga on the beach, tapas and siestas. Alas, my dwindling bank balance told a different story. I had hired a rustic villa in the mountains to run juice retreats for a few people at a time, working from dawn till dusk and doing everything myself – not exactly a sustainable business model.

A random email from an old TV contact was the reality check I needed to put the retreats – and fasting – on the map. I worked up a pitch document and decided to knock on the doors of any media person I knew to get the format made into a TV series. Thirteen knock-backs later and I finally got a "yes".

My retreats ended up becoming the subject of more than seven TV series, shown in over 22 countries around the world, which continue to be shown today.

I believe that the reason the series became such a phenomenon is that it showed, beyond a shadow of a doubt, that even dramatic health conditions are curable.

Almost a decade on, I still have people from all over the world getting in touch or attending my retreats who say that watching the series gave them hope and a new direction. Many times, over I've been told that seeing health transformed using something as simple as a fast was the nudge they needed to take action in their own lives.

# The Healthy Keto Meal Prep Cookbook with Pictures

*Bend the Rules to Lose Weight Tasting Tens of Easy-to-Prep Ketogenic Recipes On a Budget*

**By**

**Alessandro Vasquez**

# Table of Contents

# Introduction

Few aspects are as well known in nutrition research as the tremendous health advantages of low-carb and ketogenic diets. Not only can these diets increase the cholesterol, blood pressure and blood sugar, but they also reduce your appetite, promote weight control and decrease the triglycerides.

A ketogenic diet may be an interesting way to manage such disorders and could accelerate weight loss. Yet it is challenging to follow, because it may be high on red meat and other oily, dried, and salty foods that are notoriously unhealthy. We still may not know anything about the long-term consequences, presumably because it's too hard to stay with that people can't eat this way for a long time. It is also important to note that "yo-yo diets" that contribute to rapid weight loss fluctuation are correlated with increased mortality. Instead of joining in the next common diet that will last just a few weeks or months (for most people that requires a ketogenic diet), strive to accept progress that is manageable over the long term. A healthy, unprocessed diet, abundant in very colorful fruits and vegetables, lean meats, seafood, whole grains, almonds, peas, olive oil, and plenty of water seems to provide the strongest evidence for a long, healthier, vibrant existence.

If you're interested to improve your fitness, this diet book might be worth considering.

# Chapter 1: Keto Diet

The ketogenic (keto) diet is commonly known for having a diet (low crab), where the body creates ketones in the liver to be used as energy. It's alluded to by several different names – ketogenic diet, low carb diet, low carb high fat (LCHF), etc. When you consume something rich in carbohydrates, the body can release glucose and insulin.

**Glucose** is the simplest molecule for the body to transform and use as energy such that it can be preferred over some other energy source.

**Insulin** is created to process the glucose in your bloodstream by taking it across the body.

The glucose is being used as primary energy; the fats are not required and are thus processed. Usually, on a regular, higher carbohydrate diet, the body can use glucose as the key energy source. By lowering the consumption of carbohydrates, the body is induced into a condition known as ketosis. Ketosis, a normal mechanism the body initiates to help us live while food consumption is limited. During this state, we create ketones, which are formed by the oxidation of fats in the liver.

The ultimate aim of a well-controlled keto diet is to push your body into this physiological condition. We don't do this by deprivation of calories or starvation of carbohydrates.

## What Do I Eat on a Keto Diet?

To initiate a keto diet, you may want to prepare accordingly. That implies getting a viable diet plan ready a. What you consume depends on how quickly you choose to get into a ketogenic condition, i.e., ketosis. The further stringent you are on your carbohydrates (less than 25g net carbs a day), the sooner you can reach ketosis.

You want to keep your carbs limited, come more from fruits, nuts, and dairy. Don't consume some processed grains such as wheat (bread, pasta, and cereals), starch (potatoes, beans, legumes) or berries. The small exceptions to this are banana, star fruit, and berries which may be eaten in moderation.

## Do Not Eat
Grains: grain, maize, cereal, rice, etc.

Sugar: honey, maple syrup, agave, etc.

Fruit: bananas, grapes, strawberries, etc.

Tubers: yams, potatoes, etc.

## Do Eat
Meats: fish, meat, lamb, chickens, chickens, etc.

Leafy Greens: lettuce, cabbage, etc.

Vegetables:  broccoli, cauliflower, etc.

Low Fat Dairy:  strong cheeses, high-fat milk, butter, etc.

Nuts and seeds: macadamias, walnuts, sunflower seeds, etc.

Avocado and berries – raspberries, blackberries, and other low glycemic

Sweeteners:  stevia, erythritol, monk berries, and other low-carb sweeteners

Other fats:  palm oil, high-fat salad dressing, fatty fats, etc.

## Benefits of a Ketogenic Diet
Several advantages come from being on keto: from weight reduction and improved energy levels to medicinal uses. Mostly, everyone can easily profit from consuming

a low-carb, high-fat diet. Below, you'll find a concise list of the advantages you may get from a ketogenic diet.

## Weight Loss

The ketogenic diet actually utilizes your body fat as an energy source – but there are clear weight-loss advantages. On keto, your insulin (the fat-storing hormone) level drops greatly and transforms your body into a fat-burning process. Scientifically, the ketogenic diet has demonstrated better outcomes relative to low-fat and high-carb diets, also in the long run.

## Control Blood Sugar

Keto reduces blood sugar levels due to the kinds of diet you consume. Studies also suggest that the ketogenic diet is a more efficient way to treat and avoid diabetes relative to low-calorie diets.

If you're pre-diabetic or have Type II diabetes, you should strongly try a ketogenic diet. We have several readers who have had experience in their blood sugar management on keto.

## Mental Focus

Many people use the ketogenic diet primarily for improved mental output. Ketones are a perfect source of food for the brain. When you reduce carb consumption, you stop major increases in blood sugar. Together, which will help in increased attention and concentration? Studies suggest that an improved consumption of fatty acids may have affecting benefits to our brain's function.

### Increased Energy & Normalized Hunger

By providing your body a stronger and more stable energy supply, you can feel more energized throughout the day. Fats are the most powerful molecule to burn as heat. On top of that, fat is inherently more rewarding and ends up keeping us in a satiated ("full") condition for longer.

## Types of Ketogenic Diets

Many people wonder whether carbs are required to grow muscle. Actually, they're not. If you're asking this question, I will presume you know how you accumulate mass.

Your glycogen reserves will also be refilled while on a ketogenic diet. A keto diet is an effective way to grow muscle, but protein consumption is essential here. It's proposed that if you are trying to grow muscle, you could be getting in between 1.0 – 1.2g protein per lean pound of body mass. Putting muscle on can be slower on a ketogenic diet, but that's because the overall body fat is not growing as much.

If, for any reason, you need to add on body fat, too, you will accomplish your targets by various forms of a Ketogenic Diet. There are:

**Standard Ketogenic Diet (SKD):** This is the classic keto diet that everybody understands and does.

**Targeted Ketogenic Diet (TKD):** This variant is where you consume SKD but ingest a limited amount of fast-digesting carbohydrates before a workout.

**Cyclical Ketogenic Diet (CKD):** This variant of keto for bodybuilders and contests goers, usually offering one day a week to carb up and resupplies glycogen stocks.

## Common Side Effects of a Keto Diet

Here are some of the more popular side effects that one comes across when people first initiate keto. Frequently the problems contribute to dehydration or loss of micronutrients (vitamins) in the body. Be sure that you're consuming enough water (close to a gallon a day) and enjoying foods containing healthy sources of micronutrients.

### Cramps

Cramps (and, more importantly, leg cramps) are a fairly normal occurrence before beginning a ketogenic diet. It's typically happening in the morning or at night, but overall, it's a fairly small concern. It's a warning that there's a shortage of minerals, especially magnesium, in the body. Be sure you consume lots of fluid and eat salt on your meal. Using so will help reduce the lack of magnesium and get rid of the problem.

### Constipation

The most frequent source of constipation is dehydration. An easy approach is to maximize water consumption and aim to get as close to a gallon a day as possible.

Trying to make sure veggies have some fiber. Bringing in some high-quality fiber from non-starchy vegetables will fix this issue. Though if that's not enough, normally, psyllium husk powder can work or take a probiotic.

### Heart Palpitations

When switching to keto, you may find that the heart is beating both faster and slower. It's fairly normal, so don't think about it. If the condition remains, make sure that you're consuming enough liquids and eating enough salt. Usually, this is adequate to get rid of the issue right away. Though if the problem continues, it might be worth having a potassium supplement once a day.

**Reduced Physical Performance**

You can have some restrictions on your results when you start a keto diet, but it's generally only from your body transitioning to using fat, when your body changes in utilizing fat for energy, all of your power and stamina will return to normal. If you still notice issues with results, you can see benefits from taking carbs before exercising (or cycling carbs).

## Saving Money and Budgeting

A popular myth is that the ketogenic diet is more costly than most diets out there. And, though it can be a little bit more costly than eating grain-stuffed goods, it's still better than many people believe. A ketogenic diet can be more costly than a regular American diet, but it's no different than most clean eating lifestyles. That said, there are always several ways to save money when cooking keto. The key strategies to raise money are the same as in all other budgeting:

Look for offers. There's still a discount or an offer to be had on keto-friendly products out there. Usually, you can find substantial discounts in magazines and newspapers that are delivered to your home, but they can also be paired with in-store specials and manager cuts. As paired, you will save a large portion of your keto groceries.

Bulk purchase and cook. If you're somebody who doesn't want to invest a lot of time in the kitchen, this is the best in all worlds. Buying the food at volume (specifically from wholesalers) will reduce the cost per pound immensely. Plus, you can make ahead food (bulk cook chicken thighs for pre-made beef, or cook whole meals) that are used as leftovers, meaning you waste less time preparing.

Do stuff yourself. Although it's incredibly easy to purchase certain products pre-made or pre-cooked, it still contributes to the price per pound of goods. Try prepping vegetables ahead of time instead of getting pre-cut ones. Try having your stew meat from a chuck roast. Or attempt to produce your mayo and salad dressings at home. The easiest of items will operate to cut back on your overall food shopping.

## How to Reach Ketosis

Achieving ketosis is fairly simple, but it may appear complex and overwhelming for all of the details out there. Here's the bottom line about what you need to do, arranged in stages of importance:

**Restrict the sugars:** Many people prefer to only rely only on net carbohydrates. If you want better outcomes, restrict both. Aim to remain below 20g net carbs and below 35g gross carbs a day.

**Restrict the protein consumption:** Some people come over to keto from an Atkins diet and don't restrict their protein. Too much protein can contribute to lower levels of ketosis. Ideally, you ought to eat between 0.6g and 0.8g protein per pound of lean body fat. To assist with this, try using the keto calculator >

Stop thinking about fat: Fat is the main source of calories on keto – just be sure you're giving the body plenty of it. You should not lose weight on keto by malnutrition.

**Drink water:** Aim to drink a gallon of water a day. Make sure that you're hydrating and remaining compliant with the volume of water you consume. It not only helps regulate many important bodily functions, but it also helps manage hunger levels.

**Stop snacking:** Weight reduction seems to perform well because you have fewer insulin surges during the day. Unnecessary snacking can lead to stalls or delays in development.

**Start fasting:** Fasting can be a perfect tool to raise ketone levels reliably during the day. There are several different ways to go about it. Add workout in. It's a proven reality that exercise is safer. If you want to get the best out of your ketogenic diet, try putting in 20-30 minutes of workout a day. Also, only a short stroll will help control weight loss and blood sugar levels.

**Begin supplementing:** Although not normally required, supplementing can aid with a ketogenic diet.

## What the Science Tell Us about the Keto Diet

The keto diet has been used to better treat epilepsy, a condition marked by seizures, for more than 100 years. More current trials are investigating the keto diet as an effective nutritional therapy for obesity and diabetes. Clinical results on the effects of the keto diet on these health problems are exceedingly minimal. Studies on the success of the keto diet are performed with limited groups of participants. And, much of the research on Alzheimer's disease depends on testing conducted on experimental animals. To completely evaluate the protection of this eating style, further study is required. Plus, research must be performed on the long-term health implications of the keto diet. Body mass index and human metabolic rates affect how easily various people generate ketones. This suggests that certain individuals lose weight more slowly with the keto diet than others even though they are pursuing the same keto diet schedule. For this community of individuals, the keto diet may be stressful and can affect their enthusiasm for making healthy lifestyle improvements. Plus, many individuals are not willing to continue with the keto diet and gain back weight after adjusting to their former eating style.

# Chapter 2: Keto Diet Breakfast Recipes

## Keto Hot Chocolate

**YIELDS: 1**

**TOTAL TIME: 0** HOURS **20** MINS.

**INGREDIENTS**

- • 2 Tbsp. of cocoa powder, and more for flavor

- • 2 1/2 Tsp. of sugar keto (diet), (such as swerve)

- • 1 1/4 c. of Water

- • 1/4 c. of heavy cream

- • 1/4 Tsp. of Pure vanilla bean paste

- • Whipped serum, for serving

**DIRECTIONS**

1. In a small saucepan over medium-low heat, whisk together swerve, cocoa powder or about 2 Tbs. water until smooth and dissolved. Increase heat to medium, add remaining water and cream, and whisk until cook.

2. Mix the chocolate then pour into cup. Serve with whipped cream and a dusting of sugar powder.

## Keto Sausage Breakfast Sandwich

**YIELDS: 3**

**TOTAL TIME**: 0 HOURS 15 MINS

**INGREDIENTS**

- 6 large size eggs
- 2 Tbsp. of heavy cream
- Pinch of red chili flakes

- Salt (kosher)
- Finely roasted black pepper
- 1 Tbsp. of butter
- 3 slices of cheddar
- 6 packaged of sausage burgers, cooked as per box directions
- Avocado, sliced

## DIRECTIONS

1. Take a small bowl beat eggs, red chili flakes and heavy cream jointly. Season with pepper and salt. Melt the butter in fry pan at low flame. Add around one third of eggs in to pan. Add a piece of cheese in the center or let stay for 1 minute. Roll the ends of egg in to center, filling a cheese. Take out from heat and continue with leftover egg.

2. Serve eggs in 2 sausage buns with avocado.

# Keto Breakfast Cups

**YIELDS: 12**

**TOTAL TIME: 0** HOURS **40** MINS

**INGREDIENTS**

- 2 Ib. of Pork (ground)

- 1 Tbsp. thyme, finely sliced

- 2 cloves of garlic, finely chopped

- 1/2 Tsp. of Paprika

- 1/2 Tsp. of cumin, ground

- 1 Tsp. of Salt kosher

- Black pepper softly roasted

- 21/2 cup of clean minced spinach

- 1 c. of cheddar, thinly sliced

- Eggs, 12
- 1 Tbsp. of chives that are finely cut

## DIRECTIONS

1. 1 Preheat the oven at 400 degrees. Combine the thyme, ground pork, paprika, garlic, salt, and cumin in a large size cup.

2. In each muffin container, add a tiny handful of pork and push up the sides to make a cup. Split the cheese and spinach equally in cups. Break the egg and add the salt and pepper on the top of each cup. Cook for around 25 minutes until the eggs are fixed and the sausage is fried.

3. Garnish and serve with chives.

## Best-Ever Cabbage Hash Browns

**YIELDS: 2**

**TOTAL TIME: 0** HOURS **25** MINS

## INGREDIENTS

- 2 Large size eggs
- 1/2 Tsp. of garlic, powdered
- 1/2 Tsp. of  salt (kosher)
- Freshly roasted black pepper
- 2c. of cabbage that is shredded
- ¼ of small size yellow onions, finely chopped
- 1 Tbsp. of oil ( vegetable)

## DIRECTIONS

1. Whisk the garlic powder, salt, and eggs together in a large cup. Add black pepper for seasoning.  In egg mixture add onion and cabbage and toss to mix properly.

2. Heat oil in a large frying pan. Split the mixture in the pan into 4 patties and   press spatula to soften. Cook until soft and golden, around three minutes on each side.

# Chocolate Keto Protein Shake

**YIELD: 1**

**TOTAL TIME: 0** HOURS **5** MINS

**INGREDIENTS**

- 3/4 c of almond milk
- 1/2 c. of ice
- 2 Tbsp. of Butter (almond)
- 2 Tbsp. of (Sugar free) powder of cocoa
- 3 Tbsp. of keto-diet sugar substitute as per taste (such as Swerve)
- 1Tbsp. seeds of chia or more for serving
- 2 Tbsp. seeds of hemp, or more for serving
- 1/2 Tbsp. of pure vanilla (extracted)
- Salt kosher as per taste

## DIRECTIONS

1. Merge all of blending mixture and mix untill soft. Put into glass and serve with hemp seed and chia.

## Hard Boiled Egg

## YIELDS: 1

## TOTAL TIME: 0 HOURS 20 MINS

## INGREDIENTS

- 12 large size eggs

- Some water

## DIRECTIONS

1. Place the eggs in such a wide saucepan and cover them with one inch of ice water. Keep the saucepan on the burner and get it to a boil. Immediately turn off the flame and cover the saucepan. Let settle down for eleven minutes.

2. Take it out from the pan and switch it to ice water. Until serving or peeling, let it cool for 2 minutes.

## Paleo Breakfast Stacks

**YIELDS: 3**

**TOTAL TIME: 0** HOURS **30** MINS

**INGREDIENTS**

- 3 sausage buns for breakfast
- 1 avocado, finely mashed

- Salt (kosher )

- Black pepper freshly roasted

- 3 large size eggs

- Chives, (for serving)

- Hot sauce, if ordered

## DIRECTIONS

1. Cook the breakfast sausage as per the box's instructions.

2. Mash the avocado over the sausage for breakfast and season with pepper and salt.

3. Use cooking oil to spray the medium size pan then spray the interior of mason jar cover. Place the mason jar lid in the middle of the pan and crack the interior of an egg. Add pepper or salt and cook until the whites are set for 3 minutes, then remove the cover and begin to cook.

4. Place the egg on top of the avocado puree. Serve with chives and drizzle with your   favorite spicy hot sauce.

# Ham & Cheese Breakfast Roll-Ups

**YIELDS: 2**

**TOTAL TIME: 0** HOURS **20** MINS

**INGREDIENT**

- 4 large size eggs
- 1/4 c of milk
- 2 Tbsp. of finely cut chives
- Salt (kosher )
- Black pepper freshly roasted
- 1Tbsp.  of butter

- 1c. of cheddar shredded,( Split)
- 4 slices of ham

## DIRECTIONS

1. Whisk the milk, chives, and egg together in a medium cup. Add pepper or salt.
2. Melt the butter in a medium pan over low heat. Put 1/2 of the egg mixture in the pan and shift to make a thin layer that covers the whole plan.
3. Cook for two minutes. Add1/2 cup of cheddar or seal again for 2 minutes, before the cheese has melted transfer to plate, and put 2 slices of ham or rolls them. Repeat and cook with the rest of the ingredients.

## Cauliflower Toast

**YIELDS: 4 - 6**

**TOTAL TIME: 0** HOURS **45** MINS

## INGREDIENTS

- 1 cauliflower ( in medium size)
- Large size egg
- 1/2 c. of cheddar cheese (shredded)
- 1Tsp.of garlic( powdered)
- Salt (kosher)
- Black pepper freshly roasted

## DIRECTIONS

1. Set the oven at 425 degree temperature and cover the baking sheet with parchment paper. Finely chopped the cauliflower and switch to a large size cup. Set the microwave at high temperature for 8 minutes. Drain with cheesecloth and paper towels just before the mixture is dry.

2. In cauliflower cup, add the cheddar, garlic powder and egg and season with pepper and salt. Mix it until joint

3. Make a cauliflower into bread forms on prepared baking sheet and bake for 18 to 20 minutes until golden.

4. Switch to a plate cover with the appropriate topping, such as fried egg, mashed avocado, tomato, broccoli, and sausage.

# Breakfast Bacon and Egg Salad

**YIELDS: 4**

**TOTAL TIME: 0** HOURS **30** MINS

**INGREDIENTS**

**Bacon vinaigrette**

- 4 bacon (slices)
- 1 shallot, thinly sliced
- 3 Tbsp. of red wine( vinegar)
- 1 Tsp. of mustard (Dijon)
- 1/4 Tsp. of salt (kosher)
- 1/4 Tsp. of black pepper
- 4 Tbsp. of Oil

**Salad**

2   small size eggs

1 Spinach (package)

1/4 c. of crumbled feta

1 pt. of tomatoes and cherry

## DIRECTIONS

1. In a large fry pan, cook the bacon. Remove the bacon slices and put on a plate and line with towel paper to drain. Implode half of the bacon until the excess fat has drained, then cut the rest of two pieces into large pieces. Set again.

2. Making the vinaigrette: Add the shallot into the pot in which the bacon has been fried, and sauté for around 1 minute over moderate flame until golden brown. Pour the shallots into a small cup and blend with the pepper, salt, red vinegar, and mustard.  Whisk in the oil, and then add the crumbled bacon and blending to combine. Set again.

3. In the same pot, fried each egg and cook until the egg white is fixed.

4. Assemble the salad: Combine the feta, lettuce, tomatoes, cherry, spinach and the remaining sliced bacon in a large size dish. Cover with vinaigrette.

5. Place the salad in two cups and cover it with the fried egg. Immediately serve.

# Keto Blueberry Muffins

**YIELD: 1**

**TOTAL TIME: 0** HOURS **40** MINS

**INGREDIENTS**

- 2 1/2 c. of almond Flour

- 1/3 c. of Keto diet sugar (such as Swerve)

- 1 1/2 Tsp. of baking powder

- 1/2 Tsp. of baking soda

- 1/2 Tsp. salt kosher

- 1/3 c. of melted butter

- 1/3 c. of Sugar free almonds milk

- 3 large size eggs

- 1 Tsp. of pure vanilla extract

- 2/3 of c. of fresh blueberries

- ½ of lemon zest (as an option)

## DIRECTIONS

1. Preheat oven to 350° and line a 12-cup muffin pan with cupcake liners.

2. In a large bowl, whisk to combine baking powder, baking soda, almond flour, salt kosher and swerve. Whisk in eggs, vanilla, almond milk, melted butter and almond milk until just together.

3. Gently fold lemon zest (if using) and blueberries until uniformly divided. Scoop uniform quantity of butter into every cupcake liner and cook until slightly golden brown and insert a toothpick into the middle of a muffin comes out clean, 23 minutes. Let cool slightly before presenting.

# Mason Jar Omelets

**YIELDS: 2**

**TOTAL TIME: 0** HOURS **15** MINS

**INGREDIENTS**

- Nonstick cooking oil
- 4 large size eggs
- 2/3 c. of cheddar shredded
- ½ of onion, thinly sliced
- 1 Chopped capsicum
- 1/2 c. of ham (sliced)
- Salt kosher
- Freshly roasted black pepper

- 1Tbsp. of Chives that are finely sliced

## DIRECTIONS

1. Oil the nonstick baking spray into two liter mason jars.
2. Break two eggs into each jar. Between two jar divide the onion, ham capsicum, and cheese and season with pepper and salt.
3. Put cover on jar and mix until eggs are scrambled and all ingredients are mixed.
4. Remove the cover and place in the oven. Microwave for 4 minutes on low flame, and looking every 30 seconds. Garnish with chives, and serve immediately.

## Keto Fat Bombs

**YIELDS: 16**

**TOTAL TIME: 0** HOURS **30** MIN

**INGREDIENTS**

- 8 oz. of cream cheese, mitigated at room temp.
- 1/2 c. of keto diet ( peanuts) butter
- 1/4 c of (coconut oil)
- 1/4 Tsp. of salt (kosher)

- 1/2 c. of dark chocolate (keto diet) (such as Lily's)

## DIRECTIONS

1. Cover the baking sheet with a tiny parchment paper. Mix the peanut butter, salt, cream cheese and 1/4 cup of coconut oil in a medium dish. With the help of hand blender beat the mixture for around 2 minutes until all ingredients are properly mixed. Keep the dish for 10 to 15 minutes in the freezer to firm up slightly.

2. Using a tiny cookie spoon or scoop to make a Tbs. sized balls until the (peanut butter) mixture has been settled. Keep in the freezer for 5 minutes to harden.

3. Besides that, making a drizzle of chocolate: mix the cocoa powder and the leftover coconut oil in a safe microwave dish and cook for 30 seconds until completely melt. Drizzle over the balls of peanut butter and put them back in the fridge to harden for 5 minutes.

4. Keep the cover and freeze it for storage purpose.

# Cloud Eggs

**YIELDS: 4**

**TOTAL TIME: 0** HOURS **20** MINS

**INGREDIENTS**

- 8 large size eggs
- 1 c. of Parmesan, thinly sliced
- 1/2 lb. of Ham deli, diced
- Salt (kosher)
- Freshly made black pepper
- For serving, finely sliced chives

**DIRECTIONS**

1. Heat the oven at 450 °C and spread cooking oil on a large baking sheet. Separate the yolks and egg whites, yolks are keep in small cup and egg whites are keep in large cup egg whites. Use a hand blender or whisk break egg whites before stiff peaks shape and cook for 3 minutes. Fold in the ham and parmesan or season with pepper and salt.

2. Spoon the 8 mounds of egg onto the heated baking dish and indent centers to make nests. Cook for around 3 minutes, until lightly golden.

3. Spoon the egg yolk cautiously into the middle of each nest, then season with pepper or salt. Cook for around 3 minutes more until the yolks are ready.

4. Before presenting, garnish it with chives.

# Chapter 3: Keto Diet Lunch Recipes

## Cobb Egg Salad

**YIELDS: 6**

**TOTAL TIME: 0** HOURS **20** MINS

**INGREDIENTS**

- 3 Tbsp. of mayonnaise
- 3 Tbsp. of yogurt
- 2 tbsp. of vinegar with red wine
- Salt (kosher)
- Black pepper freshly roasted
- 8 hard-boiled eggs, sliced into 8 pieces, and more for garnishing.
- 8 bacon strips, fried and crumbled, and more for garnishing.

- 1 avocado, cut finely

- 1/2 c. of  blue cheese, crumbled, and more for garnishing

- 1/2 c.  of  halved cherry tomatoes, and more for garnishing

- 2 Tbsp. of  chives that are finely chopped

## DIRECTIONS

1. Mix   the yogurt,   red vinegar   and   mayonnaise   together   in   a   small cup.  Seasoning with pepper and salt.

2. Mix the avocado, bacon, eggs, pineapple, cherry tomatoes and blue cheese, softly together in a large serving cup. Gently roll in the mayonnaise coating until the all ingredients are finely coated, and then sprinkle with pepper and salt.

3. Serving with chives and supplementary toppings

# Taco Stuffed Avocado

**YIELDS: 4 - 8**

**TOTAL TIME: 0** HOURS **25** MINS

**INGREDIENTS**

- 4 large size avocados
- 1 lime juice
- 1 Tbsp. of olive oil (extra-virgin)
- 1 medium size onion, minced
- 1 lb. minced meat of beef
- 1 taco seasoning pack
- Salt (kosher)
- Blinerack pepper freshly roasted

- 2/3 of c. of chopped Mexican cheese
- 1/2 c. of chopped Lettuce
- 1/2 c. of Grape tomatoes (Sliced)
- Sour milk, for garnishing

## DIRECTIONS

1. Pit and halve the avocados halve and pit. Scoop out a bit of avocado with the help of a spoon, forming a wide layer. Dice extracted avocado and later put aside for use. Pinch the lime juice (to avoid frying!) at all the avocados.

2. Heat the oil in a medium size pan over medium heat. Add the onion and roast for around 5 minutes, until soft. Break up the meat with a wooden spatula then add ground beef and taco for seasoning. Sprinkle with pepper and salt, and roast for around 6 minutes until the beef is no more pink. Drain the fat after removing from the heat.

3. Fill up the each avocado halve with meat, then and coat with cheese, reserved avocado, tomato, onion, lettuce, and a dollop of sour cream.

# Buffalo Shrimp Lettuce Wraps

**YIELDS: 4**

**TOTAL TIME: 0** HOURS **35** MINS

**INGREDIENTS**

- 1/4 Tbsp. of butter
- 2 cloves of garlic, chopped
- 1/4 c. of Hot sauce, for example, Frank's
- 1 Tbsp. of olive oil (extra-virgin)
- 1 lbs. of Chopped and finely diced shrimp, tails (cut )
- Salt kosher
- Black pepper freshly roasted
- 1 head Romaine, different leaves, for garnishing
- 1/4 of red onion, finely minced

- 1 rib celery, finely chopped
- 1/2 c. of Crumbled blue cheese

## DIRECTIONS

1. Making the buffalo sauce: Melt the butter in a small pan. When fully melted, then add chopped garlic and simmer for 1 minute, until golden brown. Add hot sauce and stir together. Switch the heat to low whilst the shrimp is frying.

2. Making shrimp: Heat oil in a large frying pan. Put some shrimp and sprinkle with pepper and salt. Cook, turning midway, until both sides are opaque and pink, around 2 minutes on each side. Turn off the flame and add the (buffalo) sauce and toss to fill.

3. Prepare wraps: In the middle of the romaine leaf add a little scoop of shrimp, then coat with celery, blue cheese and red onion.

# Keto Broccoli Salad

**YIELDS:** 4

**TOTAL TIME: 0** HOURS **35** MINS

## INGREDIENTS

**For the salad:**

- Salt (kosher )
- 3 broccoli heads, sliced into bite-size parts
- 1/2 c. of  cheddar shredded
- 1/4 red onion, finely cut
- 1/4 c. of     almonds sliced  (baked)

- 3 bacon slices, fried and crumbled
- 2 Tbsp. of Chives that are finely cut

## For the dressing:

- 2/3 of c. of mayonnaise
- 3 Tbsp. of Vinegar (Apple Cider )
- 1 Tbsp. of Mustard dijon
- salt kosher
- Black pepper freshly roasted

## DIRECTIONS

1. Bring the 6 cups of (salted) water to a boil in a medium pot or frying pan. Prepare a big bowl of ice water while waiting for the water to heat.

2. Put some broccoli florets to the boiling water and simmer for 1 to 2 minutes, until soft. Detach with a slotted spoon, and put in the prepared ice water cup. Drain the florets in a colander while it is cold.

3. In a medium dish, whisk together the ingredients for the dressing. Season with pepper and salt to taste.

4. In a large bowl, combine all the salad ingredients and pour over the coating. Toss before the components are coated in the dressing. Refrigerate until prepared

# Keto Bacon Sushi

**YIELDS: 12**

**TOTAL TIME: 0** HOURS **30** MINS

## INGREDIENTS

- 6 bacon pieces,  (halved)

- 2 Persian cucumbers, cut finely

- 2 medium  size carrots, cut finely

- 1 avocado, in slices

- 4 oz.  of  melted cream cheese, (cooked)

## DIRECTIONS

1. Preheat oven to 400 ° degrees. Cover a baking sheet and match it with a cooling rack and aluminum foil. Put some bacon pieces in an even layer and cook for 11 to 13 minutes until mildly crisp but still pliable.

2. Mean a while, cut avocado, cucumbers, and broccoli into pieces around the width of bacon.

3. Spread an equal layer of cream cheese on each slice until the bacon is cold enough to touch it. Split up the vegetables between the bacon uniformly and put them on one side. Tightly roll up the vegetables.

4. Serve  and garnish with  sesame seeds.

## Keto Burger Fat Bombs

**YIELDS: 20**

**TOTAL TIME: 0** HOURS **30** MINS

## INGREDIENTS

- Cooking oil

- 1 lbs. of ground-based meat

- 1/2 Tsp. of Powdered garlic

- Salt Kosher

- Black pepper freshly roasted

- 2 Tbsp. of cold butter,20 (sliced)

- 2 oz. of cheddar cheese 20 (sliced)

- Lettuce berries, meant for garnishing

- For garnishing, finely sliced tomatoes

- Mustard, for garnishing

## DIRECTIONS

1. Preheat the oven at 375 °C and oil mini muffin container with cooking oil. And season the beef with garlic powder, salt, and pepper in a medium dish.

2. In the bottom of each muffin tin cup add the 1 Tsp. of beef equally, and fully covering the bottom. Place a layer of butter on top and add 1 Tsp. of beef over the butter to fully cover.

3. In each cup, place a slice of cheddar on top of the meat and place the remaining beef over the cheese to fully cover.

4. Bake for about 15 minutes, before the meat is ready. Let wait until cool.

5. Using a metal offset spoon carefully to release each burger out of the tin. Serve with salad leaves, mustard and onions.

# Keto Taco Cups

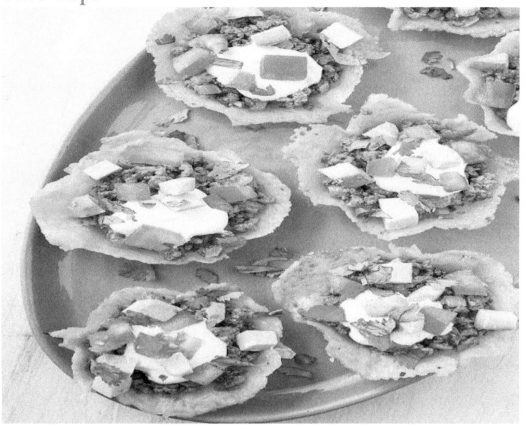

**YIELDS: 1** DOZEN

**TOTAL TIME: 0** HOURS **30** MINS

## INGREDIENTS

- 2 c. of Cheddar (Sliced) cheese
- 1 Tbsp. of Olive Oil (extra-Virgin)
- 1 small size chopped onion
- 3 cloves of garlic , finely chopped
- 1 lbs. of meat, ground
- 1 Tsp. of chili( in powdered form)
- 1/2 Tsp. of Cumin ,ground

- 1/2 tsp. of  Paprika

- Salt (kosher)

- Black pepper freshly roasted

- Sour cream, to serve

- Diced avocado, planned for serving

- Cilantro finely chopped, for serving

- Tomatoes, chopped, for garnishing

## DIRECTIONS

1. Preheat the oven to 375 ° and use parchment paper to cover a wide baking sheet. Add  2 teaspoons of cheddar a half inch away. Cook for around 6 minutes, until creamy and the edges begin to turn golden. Leave the baking sheet for a minute until cool.

2. Besides that, apply the oil in the muffin tin bottom with a cooking spray, then carefully pick up the slices of melted cheese and put them on the muffin tin bottom. Add another inverted muffin container until cool for 10 minutes. Using your hands to help shape the cheese around the twisted pan because you do not have a second muffin tin.

3. Preheat the large size pan over medium heat.  Put  the onion and simmer for around 5 minutes, mixing frequently, until soft. Whisk in the garlic, then add the ground beef to break up the beef with the help of wooden spoon. Cook for around 6 minutes, until the beef is no longer pink, and then drain the fat.

4. Place the meat back in the pan and season with cumin, chili powder, cinnamon, paprika, and pepper.

5. Move the cups of cheese into a serving bowl. Cover it with cooked ground beef and serve with cilantro, sour cream, tomatoes, and avocado.

## Copycat Chicken Lettuce Wraps

**YIELDS: 4**

**TOTAL TIME: 0** HOURS **30** MINS

**INGREDIENTS**

- 3 Tbsp. of Sauce (Hoisin)
- 2 Tbsp. Soy sauce (low-sodium)

- 2 Tbsp. vinegar from rice wine

- 1 Tbsp. of sriracha (as an option)

- 1 Tsp. oil with sesame seeds

- 1 Tbsp. olive oil (extra-virgin)

- 1 medium size chopped onion

- 2 cloves of garlic, chopped

- 1 Tbsp. of freshly coated ginger

- 1 lbs. of Chicken, ground

- 1/2 c. of drained and diced canned water chestnuts

- 2 green onions, cut finely

- Salt kosher

- Black pepper freshly roasted

- Large leafy lettuce for serving (leaves separated),

- Fried white rice, for garnishing(as an option)

## DIRECTIONS

1. Making a sauce: Whisk together the soya sauce, the hoisin sauce, the sriracha the rice wine vinegar, the Sriracha and the sesame oil in a tiny cup.

2. Heat the olive oil in a large pan over a medium-high heat. Put some onions and cook for 5 minutes until soft, then stir the garlic and ginger and cook for 1 more minute until golden brown. Add ground chicken and cook until the meat is opaque and mostly finished, trying to break up the meat with a wooden spoon.

3. Add the sauce and simmer again for 1 or 2 minutes, before the sauce is slightly reduced and the chicken is thoroughly cooked. Switch off the flame, add green onions and chestnuts and mix. Season with pepper and salt.

4. Spoon rice and add a big scoop of chicken mixture (about 1/4 cup) into the middle of each lettuce leaf (if used). Instantly serve

## Egg Roll Bowls

**YIELDS: 4**

**TOTAL TIME: 0** HOURS **35** MINS

**INGREDIENTS**

- 1 Tbsp. of oil for vegetables
- 1 clove of garlic, chopped

- 1 Tbsp. fresh ginger chopped
- 1 lbs. of pork, ground
- 1 Tbsp. of oil with sesame seeds
- 1/2 onion, cut finely
- 1 c. of Carrot( sliced)
- 1/4 green, thinly sliced (cabbage)
- 1/4 c. of soya sauce
- 1 Tbsp. of sriracha
- 1 small size green onion, finely chopped
- 1 Tbsp. of sesame seeds

## DIRECTIONS

1. Heat the vegetable oil in a large skillet over medium heat. Add the garlic and ginger and roast for 1 to 2 minutes until it is moist. Add pork and roast until there is no more pink color has been shown.

2. Place the pork and add the sesame oil to other side. Add the tomato, cabbage, and potato. Add the soy sauce and Sriracha and whisk to combine with the beef. Cook for 5 to 8 minutes, until the cabbage is soft.

3. Garnish with sesame seeds and green onions and shift the mixture to a serving bowl. Serve immediately.

# Caprese Zoodles

**YIELDS: 4**

**TOTAL TIME: 0** HOURS **25** MINS

**INGREDIENTS**

- 4 large size zucchinis

- 2 Tbsp. of olive oil (extra-virgin )

- Kosher salt

- Black pepper freshly roasted

- 2 c. of cherry tomatoes, sliced in half

- 1 c. of mozzarella cubes, cut into pieces( if large )

- 1/4 c.   fresh leaves  of basil

- 2 Tbsp. of  vinegar (balsamic)

- DIRECTIONS

1. Using a spiralizer, make zoodles with the help of zucchini.

2. In a large cup, add the zoodles mix with the olive oil, and add pepper and salt. Let them marinate for 15 minutes.

3. Add the basil, peppers, and mozzarella in zoodles and toss until mixed.

4. Drizzle and serve with balsamic.

## Best-Ever Keto Quesadillas

**YIELDS: 4**

**TOTAL TIME: 0** HOURS **35** MINS

**INGREDIENTS**

- 1 Tbsp. of olive oil ( extra-virgin)

- 1 chopped bell pepper

- 1/2of onion( yellow), chopped

- 1/2 Tsp. of chili  powdered

- Salt kosher

- Black pepper freshly roasted

- 3 c.  of Monterey jack shredded

- 3 c.  of cheddar cheese, shredded

- 4 c.  of Chicken shredded

- 1 avocado, cut thinly

- 1  green onion, finely chopped

- Sour cream, for serving

## DIRECTIONS

1. Preheat the oven to 400C and cover the parchment paper with two medium size baking sheets.

2. Heat the oil in a medium saucepan over medium heat. Season with salt, chili powder and pepper and add onion and pepper. Cook for 5 minutes, until it is tender. Transfer to a dish.

3. In a medium cup, mix the cheeses together. In the middle of both prepared baking sheets, add 1 1/2 cups of cheese mixture. Spread into an even coat and form the size of a flour tortilla into a circle.

4. Bake the cheeses for 8 to 10 minutes before they are melted and slightly golden along the sides. Add one half of  avocado slices, onion-pepper mixture, shredded chicken and avocado slices. Let it cool slowly, then use the small spoon and parchment paper and carefully fold and lift one end

of the cheese "tortilla" over the end with the topping. Return to the oven to heat for an extra 3 to 4 minutes. To make 2 more quesadillas, repeat the procedure.

5. Split each quesadilla into quarters. Before serving, garnish it with sour cream and green onion.

## Cheeseburger Tomatoes

**YIELDS: 4**

**TOTAL TIME: 0** HOURS **20** MINS

**INGREDIENTS**

- 1 Tbsp. of olive oil (extra-virgin)
- 1 medium size onion, minced

- 2 cloves of garlic, chopped

- 1 lbs. of ground-based meat

- 1 Tbsp. of ketchup

- 1 Tbsp. of mustard (Yellow)

- 4 sliced tomatoes

- Salt kosher

- Black paper freshly roasted

- 2/3 of c. of cheddar shredded

- 1/4 c. of Iceberg lettuce shredded

- 4 coins with pickles

- Seeds of sesame, for garnishing

## DIRECTIONS

1. Heat oil in a medium pan over medium heat. Add the onion and cook for approximately 5 minutes until soft, then add the garlic. Add the ground beef, split up the meat with a wooden spoon and roast for around 6 minutes until the beef is no longer pink. Drain fats. Season with pepper and salt, then add the ketchup and mustard.

2. Because they are stem-side out, tossing tomatoes. Cut the tomatoes into six slices and be cautious not to cut the tomatoes full. Fold the slices carefully. Divide the tomatoes equally with the cooked ground beef, then fill it with lettuce and cheese.

3. Add sesame seeds and pickle coins for flavoring.

# No-Bread Italian Subs

**YIELDS: 6**

**TOTAL TIME: 0** HOURS **15** MINS

**INGREDIENTS**

- 1/2 c. of mayonnaise

- 2 Tbsp. of Vinegar with red wine

- 1 Tbsp. olive oil (extra-virgin)

- 1 tiny clove of garlic, finely chopped

- 1 Tsp. of seasoning (Italian)

- 6 slices of ham

- 12 salami sliced

- 12 pepperoni, sliced

- 6 provolone slices

- 1 c. of romaine( chopped)

- 1/2 c. of red peppers (roasted)

## DIRECTIONS

1. Making a smooth Italian dressing: whisk the mustard, mayonnaise, garlic, oil, and Italian seasoning together in a small bowl until they are mixed.

2. Prepare the sandwiches: Layer a pieces of pork, two pieces of pepperoni, two pieces of salami and a piece of provolone.

3. In the center, add a handful of Romaine and a few roasted red peppers. Drizzle, with fluffy Italian sauce, then roll up and eat. Continue the procedure with the rest of the ingredients until you have 6 roll-ups.

## California Burger Bowls

**YIELDS: 4**

**TOTAL TIME: 0** HOURS **20** MINS

**INGREDIENTS**

**For the dressing:**

- 1/2 c. of olive oil (extra-virgin)
- 1/3 c. of vinegar (balsamic)
- 3Tbsp. of mustard dijon
- 2 Tsp. of. honey
- 1 clove of garlic , chopped
- Salt kosher
- Black pepper freshly roasted

**For the burger:**

- 1 lbs. of grass fed organic ground beef
- 1 Tsp. of Sauce (worcestershire)
- 1/2 tsp. of chili Powdered
- 1/2 tsp. onion Powdered
- Salt kosher
- Black pepper freshly roasted
- 1 packet of butter head lettuce
- 1 medium size red onion, sliced ( ¼)
- 1 avocado,( in pieces)
- 2 Walmart medium size tomato, thinly sliced

**DIRECTIONS**

1. Making the dressing: Whisk together the dressing components in a medium dish.

2. Making burgers: Mix beef with chili powder, (Worcestershire) sauce and onion powder in another large bowl. Season with salt and pepper and whisk until blend. Shape into 4 patties.

3. Heat a wide grill pan over medium heat and grill the onions until they are crispy and soft, around 3 minutes on at each end. Remove the grill from the pan and add the burgers. Bake until browned and fried to your taste on all ends, around 4 minutes per end for medium.

4. Assemble: Toss the lettuce with 1/2 of the dressing in a wide bowl and split between 4 bowls. Cover each with a patty of steak, tomatoes, fried onions, slices of 1/4 avocado. Drizzle and serve with the remaining dressing.

# Chapter 4: Dinner Recipes

## Keto Corned Beef & Cabbage

**TOTAL TIME: 5 HOURS 0 MINS**

**YIELDS: 6**

**INGREDIENTS:**

- 3 to 4 1bs. of corned beef
- Onions, 2 ( quartered)
- 4 stalks of, quartered crosswise celery
- 1 pack of pickling spices
- Salt ( Kosher)
- Black Pepper
- 1 medium size cabbage ( green), sliced into 2 wedges

- carrots ( 2), sliced and split into 2" part
- 1/2 c. of  Dijon mustard
- 2 Tbsp. of  ( apple cider) vinegar
- 1/4 c. of  mayonnaise
- 2 Tbsp. capers, finely sliced, plus 1 tsp. of brine
- 2 Tbsp. of   parsley, finely cut

## Directions:

1. Place corned beef, onion, celery, and pickling spices into a large pot. Add the water to cover by 2", salt with season or Pepper, and bring to the boil. Medium heat, cover, and Simmer very (tender), 3–3 1/2 hours.

2. In the meantime, whisk Dijon mustard and apple cider vinegar in a small bowl and add salt and pepper.  And in another bowl, mix capers, mayo, caper brine, and parsley. Season with salt and pepper

3. Added carrots and cabbage continue cooking for 45 minutes to 1 hour more until cabbage is soft. Remove meat, cabbage, and carrots from the pot. Piece of corned beef and season with a little more pepper and salt.

4. Present with both sauces on the side for soaking.

# Keto Fried Chicken:

## TOTAL TIME: 1 HOUR 15 MINS

## YIELDS: 6 - 8

## INGREDIENTS

## FOR THE CHICKEN

- 6 (Bone-in), chicken breasts with skin, about 4 lbs.

- Salt (Kosher)

- Black Pepper, ground and fresh

- 2 large size eggs

- 1/2 c. of heavy cream

- 3/4 c. of almond flour

- 1 1/2 c. perfectly crushed pork rinds

- 1/2 c. of grated Parmesan, fresh
- 1 Tsp. of Garlic in powder form
- 1/2 Tsp. of paprika

## FOR THE SPICY MAYO:

- 1/2 c. of Mayonnaise
- 1 1/2 Tsp. of Hot sauce

## DIRECTIONS

1. Preheat oven to 400° and cover a wide baking sheet with parchment paper. Pat dry chicken with paper towels and add salt and pepper.

2. In a small bowl, mix together eggs and heavy cream. In another small dish, mix almond flour, pork rinds, Parmesan, garlic powder, and paprika. Add salt and black pepper.

3. Work at one time, soak the chicken in egg mix, then in the almonds flour mix, pressing to cover. Put the chicken on the lined baking dish.

4. Bake till chicken is gold and internal temp exceeds 165°, about 45 minutes.

5. In the meantime, produce dipping sauce: In a medium dish, mix mayonnaise and hot sauce. Add more hot sauce based on desired spiciness amount.

6. Serve chicken warm with dipping sauce.

# Garlic Rosemary Pork Chops:

**TOTAL TIME: 0 HOURS 30 MINS**

**YIELDS: 4**

**INGREDIENTS:**

- 4 pieces of pork loin
- Salt ( kosher)
- Black pepper freshly roasted
- 1Tbsp. of Freshly chopped rosemary
- 2 Garlic cloves, minced
- 1/2 c (1 stick) of butter melted

- 1 Tbsp. of Extra-virgin (olive oil)

## DIRECTIONS:

1. Preheat the oven to 375 degrees. With salt and black pepper, season the pork chops generously.

2. Mix the honey, rosemary, and garlic together in a shallow dish. Only put back.

3. Heat the olive oil in an oven-safe skillet over (medium-high) heat and add the pork chops. Sear until golden for 4 minutes, flip and bake for a further 4 minutes. Pork chops are appropriately coated with garlic butter for 10-12 minutes.

4. Add more garlic butter to serve.

# Keto Bacon Sushi

**TOTAL TIME: 0 HOURS 30 MINS**

**YIELDS: 12**

**INGREDIENTS:**

- 6 bacon strips, cut in half
- 2 cucumbers (Persian), cut thin
- 2 carrots (medium), cut thinly
- 1 (avocado), in slices
- 4 oz. (Creamy) cheese, cooked, soft
- Seeds of sesame (garnish)

**DIRECTIONS:**

1. Preheat the oven to 400 degrees. Line a baking sheet and match with a (cooling rack) with (aluminum) foil. Lay bacon half with an even surface and cook for 11 to 13 minutes unless mildly crispy but always pliable.

2. In the meantime, split the bacon's size into pieces of cucumbers, broccoli, and avocado.

3. Spread an equal surface of cream cheese from each strip until the bacon is cold enough to touch it. Divide the vegetables into the bacon equally and put them in one hand. Strictly roll up the vegetables.

4. Season with and serve the sesame seeds.

## Keto Chicken Parmesan

**TOTAL TIME: 0 HOURS 55 MINS**

**YIELDS: 4**

**INGREDIENTS:**

- 4 boneless without skin breasts of chicken
- Kosher salt
- 1c. of Almond Flour
- 3 big, beaten eggs
- 3 c. of Parmesan, freshly grated, and much more for serving
- 2 Tsp. of Powdered garlic
- 1 1/2 c. of Mozzarella Sliced
- 1 Tsp. of onion in powdered form
- 2 Tsp. of Oregano dried
- Oil for vegetables
- 3/4 c. Sugar-free, low-carb tomato sauce
- Fresh leaves of basil for topping

**DIRECTIONS**

1. Preheat the oven to 400 degrees. Halve the chicken breasts crosswise with a sharp knife. Season the chicken with salt and pepper on both sides.

2. Put the almond flour and eggs in 2 different shallow cups. Combine the parmesan, garlic (powder), onion (powder), and oregano in the third shallow dish. With salt and pepper, season.

3. Dip the chicken cutlets into the almond flour, then the eggs, the Parmesan mixture, and push to cover.

4. Heat 2 teaspoons of oil in a large skillet. Add chicken and roast, 2 to 3 minutes on each hand, until golden and cooked through. Function as required in batches, inserting more oil as appropriate.

5. Move the fried cutlets to a 9-inch-x-13-inch baking dish, distribute the tomato sauce uniformly over each cutlet, and finish with the mozzarella.

6. Bake for 10 to 12 minutes before the cheese melts. If needed, broil for 3 minutes until the cheese is golden.

7. Until eating, top with basil and more Parmesan.

## Tuscan Butter Shrimp

**TOTAL TIME: 0 HOURS 55 MINS**

**YIELDS: 4**

**INGREDIENTS**

- 2 tbsp. of olive oil extra-virgin
- 1 lb. deveined, peeled, lobster and tails cut
- salt (kosher)
- Black pepper freshly roasted
- 3 tbsp. of Butter
- 3 garlic cloves, minced
- 1 1/2 c. of halved tomatoes with cherry
- 3 c. of spinach for kids
- 1/2 c. of heavy cream
- 1/4 c. of Parmesan, finely grated
- 1/4 c. of thinly cut basil
- Lemon wedges meant for serving as an option

## DIRECTIONS

1. Heat oil in a frying pan over medium heat. Season the shrimp with salt and pepper all over. Add the shrimp and sear until the underside is golden, around 2 minutes, and then turn until opaque, until the oil is shimmering but still not burning. Remove and set aside from the skillet.

2. Lower the heat to mild and add some butter. When the butter is melted, stir in the garlic and simmer for around 1 minute, until fragrant. Sprinkle with salt and substitute the cherry tomatoes. Cook until the tomatoes start to burst, then add the spinach and cook until the spinach begins to wilt.

3. Stir in the heavy cream, basil and parmesan cheese and carry the mixture to a boil. Reduce the heat to low and boil for around 3 minutes before the sauce is significantly reduced.

4. Place the shrimp back in the pan and mix to blend. Cook unless shrimp is cooked through, garnish with more basil, and squeeze lemon on top before eating.

## Zoodle Alfredo with Bacon

**TOTAL TIME: 0 HOURS 20 MINS**

**YIELDS: 4**

**INGREDIENTS:**

- 1/2 lb. of Chopped bacon
- 1 minced shallot,
- 2 garlic cloves, minced

- 1/4 c. of Black Alcohol, White Wine
- 1 1/2 c. of heavy cream
- 1/2 c. of Parmesan( cheese) grated, but mostly for garnishing
- 1 pack of zucchini (noodles) (16 oz.)
- Kosher Salt
- Black pepper freshly roast

## DIRECTIONS

1. Cook the bacon until crisp, 8 minutes, in a wide saucepan over medium heat. Drain it on a tray lined with paper towels.

2. Pour all but 2 teaspoons of (bacon); then shallots are included. Cook until tender, around 2 minutes, and then add garlic and cook for about 30 seconds until it is fragrant. Add wine and cook before half the quantity is depleted.

3. Connect the heavy cream to the mixture and get it to a boil. Lower the flame and stir in the Parmesan cheese. Cook for about 2 minutes, until the sauce, has thick somewhat. Add the zucchini (noodles) and toss in the sauce until thoroughly covered. Take the heat off and stir in the fried bacon.

# Keto Chicken Soup

**TOTAL TIME: 1 HOUR 0 MINS**

**YIELDS: 4 - 6**

**INGREDIENTS:**

- 2 tbsp. Oil for vegetables
- 1 medium onion, minced
- 5 garlic cloves, crushed
- 2" Fresh ginger bit, sliced
- 1 tiny cauliflower, sliced into florets
- 3/4 Tsp. smashed flakes of red pepper
- 1 medium carrot, on a bias, peeled and thin slices
- 6 c. low-sodium broth of poultry

- 1 celery stem, thinly sliced
- 2 skinless, boneless breasts of chicken
- For garnish, finely cut parsley

## DIRECTIONS

1. Heat oil in a big pot over low heat. Add the carrot, ginger, and garlic. Cook before the browning stops.

2. In the meantime, pulse cauliflower before it is split into rice-sized granules in a food processor. Return the cauliflower to the pot with the onion mixture and cook for around 8 minutes over medium-high heat until golden.

3. Bring to a boil and incorporate pepper flakes, onions, celery and chicken (broth). Add the chicken breasts and cook gently for around 15 minutes before they hit a temp of 165 ° C. Remove from the pan, leave to cool and shred until cool enough to treat. Meanwhile, proceed to cook, 3 to 5 minutes more, until the vegetables are soft.

4. Apply the (Shredded) chicken back to the broth and cut the ginger from the bath. Season with salt and pepper to taste, then garnish before serving with parsley.

# Foil Pack Grilled Salmon with Lemony Asparagus

**TOTAL TIME: 0** HOURS **20** MINS

**YIELDS: 4**

**INGREDIENTS:**

- 20 spears of asparagus, cut
- 4 6-oz. Skin-on fillets of salmon
- 4Tbsp. of Butter, break
- 2 lemons, cut
- Kosher salt
- Black pepper freshly roasted
- Broken dill (fresh), for season

**DIRECTIONS:**

1. On a hard floor lie two bits of foil. Put on the foil five spears of asparagus and finish with a salmon fillet, 1 tablespoon of butter, and two lemon slices. Cover loosely, and repeat for the rest of the ingredients and you'll have a limit of four sets.

2. High Heat Barbecue. To fry and barbecue, apply foil packets until salmon is cook through and asparagus is soft for about 10 minutes.

3. Sprinkle and mix with dill.

## Garlicky Shrimp Zucchini Pasta

**TOTAL TIME: 1 HOUR 50 MINS**

**YIELDS: 4**

**INGREDIENTS**

- 1/4 c. Of olive oil extra-virgin
- 1/4 c. the Juice in Lemons

- Kosher (salt)
- 1 head (cauliflower), cut leaves and trimmed stem such that cauliflower lies flat but still intact
- 1 (10-oz.) box of frozen (spinach), thawed, stretched out and sliced with water
- 2 big, beaten eggs
- 4 green onions, cut thinly
  - 2 cloves of garlic, minced
  - 3/4 c. of cheddar Shredded
  - 4 oz. of soft and cube white cheese
  - 1/2 c. panko a panko
  - 1/4 c. of parmesan Rubbed
  - 1 lb. of bacon thinly cut

## DIRECTIONS

1. Preheat the oven to 450 degrees. In a big kettle, put eight cups of water, oil, lemon juice and 2 tablespoons of salt to a boil. Add the cauliflower and get it to a simmer again. To hold it submerged, reduce it to a gentle simmer and put a plate on top of the cauliflower. Simmer for around 12 minutes before a knife is quickly inserted into the middle.

2. Transfer the cauliflower to a narrow rimmed baking sheet using 2 slotted spoons or a mesh spider. Only let it cool.

3. In the meanwhile, add lettuce (eggs, green onions, garlic, cheddar, cream cheese, panko, and parmesan cheese) and placed a 3/4-inch tip in a piping bag.

4. Place on a rimmed baking sheet with cooled cauliflower stem side up. Pipe filling of florets between stalks. Flip down the side of the cauliflower stem,

and then spread bacon strips, only slightly overlapping strips, over the cauliflower, tucking strip ends into the cauliflower bottom.

5. Roast, halfway through the spinning pan, before golden all over, maybe 30 minutes.

## Cajun Parmesan Salmon

**TOTAL TIME: 0 HOURS 45 MINS**

**YIELDS: 4**

**INGREDIENTS:**

- 1 tbsp. Olive oil (extra-virgin)
- 4 (4-oz.) Salmon fillets (preferably wild)
- 2 Tsp. Seasoning the Cajun
- 2 Tbsp. of Butter

- 3 garlic cloves, minced
- 1/3 c. Low-sodium( chicken) or soup with vegetables
- Juice of 1 lemon
- 1 Tbsp. of honey
- 1 Tbsp. Freshly sliced parsley, with more for garnishing
- 2Tbsp. Parmesan, finely chopped
- Slices of lemon, for serving

## DIRECTIONS

1. Heat oil in a frying pan over medium heat. Season the salmon with 1 tsp. of Cajun pepper and seasoning, then apply the skin-side-up to the skillet. Cook the salmon for around 6 minutes before it is intensely brown, then turn and cook for 2 more minutes. Transfer to a dish.

2. To the skillet, apply butter and garlic. Stir in the Broth, lemon juice, sugar, remaining Cajun seasoning teaspoon (parsley), and parmesan when the butter has melted. Take the combination to a boil.

3. Lower the heat to mild and return the salmon to the skillet. Simmer for 3 or 4 more minutes before the sauce is decreased, and the salmon is fried.

4. Apply slices of lemon to the pan and eat.

# Beef Tenderloin:

**TOTAL TIME: 1** HOUR **50** MINS

**YIELDS: 4**

**INGREDIENTS**

**FOR BEEF:**

- 1/2 c. Olive oil (extra-virgin)
- 2 Tbsp. Vinegar (Balsamic)
- 2 Tbsp. Mustard, whole grain
- Thyme(fresh), 3 sprigs
- 3 rosemary sprigs, fresh
- 1 bay leaf

- 2 garlic cloves, crushed
- 2 tbsp. of honey
- 1 (2-lb.) tenderloin beef
- 1 Tsp. salt, Kosher
- 1 Tsp. Black pepper, roasted, fresh
- 1 Tsp. The Dried( Rosemary)
- 1 garlic clove, minced
- **SAUCE FOR YOGURT**
- 1/2 c. Yogurt (Greek)
- 1/4 c. Sour milk, sour cream
- 1 Tsp. Horseradish prepared
- 1/2 lemon extract
- Kosher salt

## DIRECTIONS

1. Mix the vinegar, oil, thyme, mustard, rosemary, crushed garlic, bay leaf, and honey together in a wide container. Return the meat to the package, cover with plastic wrap, and marinate for 1 hour or up to one day in the refrigerator. Optional: Before frying, get the tenderloin to room temperature.

2. Preheat the oven to around 450C. Line an aluminum foil rimmed baking sheet and fit a wire rack inside. Strip the marinade from the tenderloin and wipe it dry with paper towels. Add salt, pepper, rosemary, and minced garlic to season all over and put on the rack.

3. Roast until baked to your taste, around 20 minutes for special occasions. Until slicing, let it rest for 5 to 10 minutes.

4. Meanwhile, render the sauce: whisk the milk, sour cream, horseradish and lemon juice together in a medium container, and season with salt.

5. Slice the tenderloin and eat it on the side with sauce.

## Baked Cajun Salmon

**TOTAL TIME: 0 HOURS 30 MINS**

**YIELDS: 4**

**INGREDIENTS**

- 1/2 large size white onion, cut thinly

- bell pepper (red), cut thinly

- 1 thinly cut orange bell pepper

- cloves of thinly sliced garlic

- Salt (kosher)

- Black Pepper, fresh, ground

- Three Tbsp. of Olive Oil (Extra-Virgin)

- 1 Tbsp. of thyme in dry form

- 1 Tbsp. of seasoning (Cajun)

- 2 Tsp. Of tweet paprika

- Tsp. of powdered garlic

- 6-oz. Filets of Salmon

## DIRECTIONS:

1. Preheat the oven to 400 degrees. Stir in the onions, pepper and garlic on a broad baking dish. Season with pepper and salt and toss with gasoline.

2. Prepare a spice mix: mix together thyme, Cajun seasoning, and paprika and garlic powder in a small cup.

3. On a baking sheet, put the salmon, top the bits with the seasoning mixture and rub them all over the salmon.

4. Bake for 20 minutes until the vegetables and salmon are soft and cooked properly.

# Chapter 5: Deserts and Snacks Recipes

## Keto Sugar-Free Cheesecake

**TOTAL TIME: 8 HOURS 0 MINS**

**YIELDS: 8 - 10**

**INGREDIENTS:**

- 1/2 c. of almond flour
- 1/2 c. Flour of coconut
- 1/4 c. of coconut, shredded
- 1/2 c. (1 stick) of melted butter
- 3 (8-oz.) cream cheese blocks, soft to room temp
- 16 oz. of sour cream ( room temperature)
- 1 Tbsp. of stevia

- 2 Tsp. a sample of pure vanilla
- 3 large size eggs, at room temperature
- Strawberries, diced, for serving

## DIRECTIONS

1. Heat the oven to 300 degrees. Create the crust: Oil a spring pan of 8 or 9 inches and coat the bottom and sides with foil. Mix the rice, coconut, and butter together in a medium dish. Push the crust towards the bottom and the sides of the prepared pan somewhat upwards. When you prepare the filling, put the pan in the fridge.

2. Prepare the filling: mix together the cream cheese and sour cream in a large bowl, then whisk in the stevia and vanilla. One at a time, add the eggs, combining after each addition. Layer the filling over the crust uniformly.

3. Put the cheesecake in a deep roasting pan and set it on the oven's center rack. Pour sufficient boiling water carefully into the roasting pan to come halfway up the spring type pan's sides. Bake for 1 hour to 1 hour 20 minutes, until the middle jiggles just slightly. Switch off the oven, but allow the cake to cool steadily for an hour in the oven with the door partially closed.

4. Remove the pan from the boiling water, remove the foil, and then let it cool for at least five hours or overnight in the refrigerator. Slice with the strawberries and garnish.

# Keto Chocolate Chip Cookies

## TOTAL TIME: 0 HOURS 30 MINS

## YIELDS: 18

## INGREDIENTS:

- 2 large size eggs

- 1/2 c (1 stick) of butter that has melted

- 2 Tbsp. of heavy milk to heavy cream

- 2 Tsp .pure extract of vanilla

- 2 3/4 c. of almond flour

- 1/4 Tsp. salt, kosher

- 1/4 c. Sugar granulated keto-friendly (such as swerve)

- 3/4 c. Chips of dark chocolate (such as lily's)

- cooking mist

## DIRECTIONS

1. Preheat 350° in the oven. Mix the egg with the sugar, vanilla and heavy cream in a big dish. Add the almond flour, salt and swerve to the mixture.

2. Fold in the cookie batter with the chocolate chips. Shape the mixture into 1" balls and arrange 3" apart on baking sheets lined with parchment. Flatten the balls with cooking spray on the bottom of a glass that has been oiled.

3. Bake for around 17 to 19 minutes until the cookies are softly golden.

## Keto Chocolate Mug Cake

**TOTAL TIME: 0 HOURS 5 MINS**

**YIELDS: 1**

## INGREDIENTS:

- 2 Tbsp. of  Butter

- 1/4 c. of almond flour

- 2 Tbsp. of powdered cocoa

- 1 large size egg, beaten

- 2 Tbsp. of chocolate chips that are keto-friendly, (such as Lily's)

- 2 Tbsp. of Swerve, Granulated

- 1/2 Tsp. of  baking powder

- A pinch of Kosher salt

- For serving, whipped cream (1/4 c.)

## DIRECTIONS

1. Put the butter in a microwave-safe mug and heat for 30 seconds before it is melted. Except for whipped cream, add the remaining ingredients and stir until thoroughly mixed. Cook until the cake is set, but always fudgy, for 45 seconds to 1 minute.

2. Serve with whipped cream.

# Keto Ice Cream

**TOTAL TIME: 8 HOURS 15 MINS**

**YIELDS: 8**

**INGREDIENT:**

- 2 cans of coconut milk (15-oz.)

- 2 c. of heavy cream

- 1/4 c. Swerve the Sweetener of the Confectioner

- 1 Tsp. of pure vanilla

- A pinch of Kosher salt

**DIRECTIONS**

1. In the refrigerator, chill the coconut milk for at least 3 hours, preferably overnight.

2. To make whipped coconut: pour coconut cream into a big bowl, keep liquid in the bowl and beat the coconut cream until very smooth using a hand mixer. Only put back.

3. Make the whipped cream: Using a hand mixer in a separate big bowl (or a stand mixer in a bowl), beat heavy cream until soft peaks shape. Beat in the vanilla and sweetener.

4. Fold the whipped (coconut) into the whipped cream, and then add the mixture to the loaf plate.

5. Freeze for about 5 hours until it is firm.

## Keto Hot Chocolate

**TOTAL TIME: 0 HOURS 10 MINS**

**YIELDS: 1 CUP**

**INGREDIENTS:**

- 2 Tbsp. Powder of unsweetened chocolate, and more for garnishing

- 2 1/2 Tsp. of sugar that is keto-friendly, such as Swerve

- 1 1/4 c. Aquatic Water

- 1/4 c. Heavy milk to heavy cream

- 1/4 Tsp. of pure vanilla

- Whipped(milk),for serving

**DIRECTIONS:**

1. Whisk together the swerve, chocolate, and about 2 teaspoons of water in a shallow pan over medium heat until smoother and dissolve. Increases heat to low, add the remaining cream and water and whisk until heated regularly.

2. Attach the vanilla, and spill it into a cup. Represent with (whipped) cream and chocolate powder dusting.

## Keto Peanut Butter Cookies

**TOTAL TIME: 1 HOUR 30 MINS**

**YIELDS: 22**

**INGREDIENTS**

- 1 1/2c. of smooth peanut butter, unsweetened, melted (plus more for drizzling)
- 1 c. Flour of coconut
- 1/4 c. Keto-friendly brown sugar packets, such as Swerve
- 1 Tsp. of pure vanilla
- Pinch of Kosher salt
- 2 c. of melted keto-friendly dark chocolate chips, including Lily's,
- 1 Tbsp. of Cream (Coconut )
- 

**DIRECTIONS**

1. Combine the sugar, coconut flour, peanut butter, salt, and vanilla in a medium dish. Until smooth, stir.
2. Line the parchment paper with a baking sheet. Shape the mixture into circles using a small cookie scoop, then push down gently to flatten slightly and position it on the baking sheet. Freeze until strong, roughly 1 hour.
3. Whisk the melting chocolate and coconut oil together in a medium dish.
4. Dip peanut butter rounds in chocolate using a fork until fully covered and then return to the baking sheet. Drizzle with much more peanut butter, and freeze for around 10 minutes before the chocolate is set.
5. Only serve it cold. In the fridge, put some leftovers.

# Chocolate Keto Cookies

## TOTAL TIME: 0 HOURS 25 MINS

## YIELDS: 11

## INGREDIENTS

- 2 1/2 Tbsp. of butter

- 3 Tbsp. of chocolate chips with keto, split

- 1large size egg

- 1 Tsp. of pure vanilla

- 2/3 of c. Almond Flour Blanched

- 1/3 c. of swerve Confectioners

- 3 1/2 Tbsp. Unsweetened dark chocolate powder

- 1/2 Tsp. Powder used for baking

- Pinch of Kosher salt

## DIRECTIONS

1. Preheat the oven to 325 degrees. Add butter and half of the (chocolate chips) into a medium-sized dish. Microwave for 15 to 30 seconds, only enough time to melt the chocolate and butter mildly. Until a chocolate sauce emerges, mix the two together.

2. Attach and whisk the egg in a tiny dish before the yolk mixes with the whites. When it's finished, add the chocolate syrup to the bowl with the egg and vanilla extract. Again, blend.

3. To finish the cookies, add the majority of the dry ingredients, save some of the chocolate chips. Mix until it shapes a mass of chocolate cookie dough.

4. To make 11 equal-sized cookies, use a cookie spoon (or a tablespoon). Attach the cookie to a baking parchment paper and top the remainder of the chocolate chips with each cookie. In either a spoon or a spatula, flatten each cookie.

5. For 8 to 10 minutes, roast. When they come out of the oven, they should be very soft, but don't worry, this is natural!

6. Let the cookies on the baking sheet cool off. They can set up and firm up while they cool up.

7. When the leftovers are cooled, enjoy them and store them in an airtight jar in the refrigerator.

# Walnut Snowball Cookies:

**TOTAL TIME: 1 HOUR 5 MINS**

**YIELDS: 15**

**INGREDIENTS**

- 1/2 c. (1 stick) of butter that has melted

- 1 large size egg

- 50 drops of stevia liquid (about 1/4 tsp.)

- 1/2 tsp. of pure vanilla

- 1 c. With walnuts

- 1/2 c. Flour of coconut, plus 1 or 2 tbsp. For rolling, more

- 1/2 c. of swerve Confectioners

## DIRECTIONS

1. Preheat the oven to 300 ° and use parchment paper to cover a baking sheet. In a large bowl, mix the melted butter, egg, vanilla extract, stevia and set aside.

2. In a food processor, add the walnuts and pulse until ground. In a medium bowl, pour the walnut flour and add the coconut flour and 1/4 cup Swerve and press until mixed.

3. Add the dry mixture to the wet in two sections and whisk to blend. The dough should be soft but strong enough at this stage to shape hand-made balls without sticking to your hands. If the quality is not right, add 1 to 2 tablespoons of extra (coconut) flour and mix.

4. Create 15 balls of the same size and place them on a lined baking sheet. In the microwave, they would not disperse.

5. For 30 minutes, roast.

6. Enable 5 minutes to settle, and then in the remaining 1/4 cup Swerve, roll the (still warm) spheres.

7. Put them back on the parchment paper and give another 20 to 30 minutes to cool fully before feeding.

# Keto Tortilla Chips

## TOTAL TIME: 0 HOURS 35 MINS

## YIELDS: 4 - 6

## INGREDIENTS

- 2 c. of Mozzarella cheese, Sliced
- 1 c. of almond flour
- 1 Tsp. salt, Kosher
- 1 Tsp. of garlic powder
- 1/2 Tsp. Powdered chili
- Black pepper freshly ground

## DIRECTIONS

1. Preheat the oven to 350 degrees. Top the parchment paper with two wide baking sheets.

2. Melt the mozzarella in a secure microwave bowl for around 1 minute and 30 seconds. Add the almond flour, cinnamon, chili powder, garlic powder, black pepper and a few pieces. Use both hands to moisten the dough a couple of times before it forms a smooth shape.

3. Place the dough between two parchment paper sheets and stretch it out into a 1/8' wide rectangle. Break the dough into triangles using a knife or a pizza cutter.

4. Spread the chips on lined baking sheets and bake for 12 to 14 minutes until the sides are golden and begin to crisp.

## Keto Burger Fat Bombs

**TOTAL TIME: 0 HOURS 30 MINS**

**YIELDS: 20**

**INGREDIENTS:**

- Cooking mist
- 1 lb. of meat, ground
- 1/2 tsp. powder in garlic form
- salt (kosher)
- Black pepper freshly ground
- 2 tbsp. Cold butter, 20 bits of sliced butter
- 2 oz. Split into 20 bits of cheddar,
- Lettuce berries meant for serving
- For serving, finely sliced tomatoes
- Mustard, to serve

**DIRECTIONS**

1. Preheat the oven to 375 °C and oil the cooking spray with a mini muffin tin. Season the beef with salt, garlic powder and pepper in a medium dish.

2. Place 1 teaspoon of beef equally, covering the bottom entirely, into the bottom of each muffin tin cup. Place a slice of butter on top and press 1 teaspoon of beef over the butter to cover full.

3. In each cup, place a slice of cheddar on top of the meat and force the remaining beef over the cheese to cover it fully.

4. Bake for about 15 minutes before the meat is ready. Let yourself cool somewhat.

5. Using a metal offset spatula carefully to release each burger out of the tin. Serve with onions, salad leaves, and mustard.

# Jalapeño Popper Egg Cups

## TOTAL TIME: 0 HOURS 45 MINS

## YIELDS: 12

## INGREDIENTS:

- 12 strips of bacon
- 10 eggs (large)
- 1/4 c. of sour milk,
- 1/2 c. Cheddar Shredded
- 1/2 c. Mozzarella Sliced
- 2( jalapeños), 1 sliced thinly and 1 finely chopped
- 1 Tsp. Powdered of garlic
- salt(kosher)
- Black pepper freshly ground

- Cooking spray, nonstick

## DIRECTIONS

1. Preheat the oven to 375 degrees. Over medium heat, (cook bacon) in a broad skillet until well browned but always pliable. Put aside to drain on a paper towel-lined pan.

2. Whisk the eggs, sour cream, cheese, minced jalapeño and garlic in powder form together in a big bowl. With salt and pepper, season.

3. Oil a muffin tin with the aid of nonstick cooking oil. Line each well with one bacon strip, then pour each muffin cup with egg mixture until around two-thirds of the way through to the end. Cover each muffin with a slice of jalapeño.

4. Bake for 20 minutes until the eggs do not look moist anymore. Before withdrawing them from the muffin pan, cool slightly.

## Keto Frosty

## TOTAL TIME: 0 HOURS 45 MINS

### YIELDS: 4

## INGREDIENTS

- 1 1/2 c. Heavy cream whipping
- 2 Tbsp. Unsweetened powder of cocoa
- 3 Tbsp. Sweetener for (keto-friendly) powdered sugar, such as a Swerve
- 1 Tsp. of pure vanilla
- Pinch of Kosher salt

## DIRECTIONS

1. Combine the milk, sugar, sweetener, vanilla, and salt in a wide pot. Beat the mixture until rigid peaks shape, and use a hand blender or (the whisk attachment of a stand mixer). Mix the scoops into a Ziploc container and ice for 30 to 35 minutes before they're frozen.
2. Break the tip off an edge of the Ziploc container and pour it into dishes to eat.

# Bacon Guac Bombs

**TOTAL TIME: 0 HOURS 45 MINS**

**YIELDS: 15**

**INGREDIENTS:**

2 bacon strips, fried and crumbled

## For guacamole

- 2 pitted, sliced, and mashed avocados
- 6 oz. of Cream cheese, cooked, softened
- 1 lime juice
- 1 clove of garlic, minced
- 1/4 of red onion, minced
- 1 small jalapeno (seeded if less fire is preferred), chopped
- 2 Tbsp. Cilantro, freshly sliced

- 1/2 Tsp. of cumin seeds

- 1/2 Tsp. Powdered of chili

- salt(kosher)

- Black pepper freshly ground

## DIRECTIONS

1. Combine all the guacamole products in a big bowl. Stir unless mostly smooth, and add salt and pepper (some pieces are OK). Put in the freezer for 30 minutes to firm up rapidly.

2. On a wide tray, put crumbled bacon. Scoop the guacamole mix and put in the bacon, utilizing a little cookie scoop. Roll in the bacon to coat. Repeat before you've used both the bacon and guacamole. Store in refrigerator.

## Avocado Chips

**TOTAL TIME: 0 HOURS 40 MINS**

**YIELDS: 15**

**INGREDIENTS**

- 1 large ripe avocado
- 3/4 c. Freshly grated parmesan
- 1 tsp. Lemon juice
- 1/2 tsp. Garlic powder
- 1/2 tsp. Italian seasoning
- Kosher salt
- Freshly ground black pepper

**DIRECTIONS**

1. Preheat oven to 325° and line two baking sheets with parchment paper. In a medium bowl, mash avocado with a fork until smooth. Stir in parmesan, lemon juice, garlic powder, and Italian seasoning. Season with salt and pepper.

2. Place heaping teaspoon-size scoops of mixture on baking sheet, leaving about 3" apart between each scoop. Flatten each scoop to 3" wide across with the back of a spoon or measuring cup. Bake until crisp and golden, about 30 minutes, then let cool completely. Serve at room temperature.

## Rosemary Keto Crackers

**TOTAL TIME: 1 HOUR 0 MINS**

**YIELDS: 140**

**INGREDIENTS**

- 2 1/2 c. almond flour

- 1/2 c. coconut flour

- 1 tsp. ground flaxseed meal

- 1/2 tsp. dried rosemary, chopped

- 1/2 tsp. onion powder

- 1/4 tsp. kosher salt

- 3 large eggs

- 1 tbsp. extra-virgin olive oil

## DIRECTIONS

1. Preheat oven to 325° and line a baking sheet with parchment paper. In a large bowl, whisk together flours, flaxmeal, rosemary, onion powder, and salt. Add eggs and oil and mix to combine. Continue mixing until dough forms a large ball, about 1 minute.

2. Sandwich dough between 2 pieces of parchment and roll to ¼" thick. Cut into squares and transfer to prepared baking sheet.

3. Bake until golden, 12 to 15 minutes. Let cool before storing in a resalable container.

# Conclusion

A ketogenic diet could be an alternative for certain people who have experienced trouble losing weight with other approaches. The exact ratio of fat, carbohydrate, and protein that is required to attain health benefits can differ among individuals due to their genetic makeup and body structure. Therefore, if one decides to start a ketogenic diet, it is advised to meet with one's physician and a dietitian to closely track any metabolic adjustments since beginning the treatment and to develop a meal schedule that is specific to one's current health problems and to avoid food shortages or other health risks. A dietitian can also have advice on reintroducing carbs after weight reduction is accomplished.

# The 15-Day Keto Fasting Cookbook

*A Sophisticated Mix of Low-Carb Recipes to Activate Ketosis and Autophagy for Life-Long Intermittent Fasting*

**By**

**Alessandro Vasquez**

# Table of Contents

# Introduction

Given the multiple kinds of diets you have probably read about in your life, you are likely to have a few fresh ones. Perhaps one amongst them may be the Ketogenic Diet, commonly known as the Keto Diet, which is a low-carbohydrate, high-fat regimen.

The idea behind the high-fat, low-carbohydrate ratio is that instead of carbs, the body would depend on fats for nutrition, and hence the body would become leaner as a consequence of getting less fat contained throughout the body.

Ideally, the Keto Diet would encourage the body to achieve ketosis or a metabolic condition where the carbs are ketones, which are fats that are burned for energy rather than glucose. Many who embrace the Keto Diet often eat only the correct amount of protein on a regular basis that the body requires. The Keto Diet does not rely on measuring calories, compared to any of the other diets that occur. Instead, the emphasis is on the food's fat, proteins and carbohydrates make-up, as well as the weight of the servings.

But what contributed to the Keto Diet being created?

In hopes of discovering a cure for seizures, a Mayo Clinic physician by the name of Russell Wilder invented the Ketogenic Diet back in 1924. Since going on this diet, many people who have epilepsy and other disorders have reported a substantial reduction in their symptoms. This procedure goes back to Ancient Greece when physicians would change the diets of their patients and even make them rapidly push their bodies into hunger mode.

The Ketogenic Diet is a much better way for the body to reach the fasting mode without completely depriving the body of food. However, to this day, no one understands precisely why the Ketogenic Diet is so effective in treating those who have epilepsy, autism, and other identified diseases.

The high-fat, low-carbohydrate combination might be a normal meal for those on the Ketogenic Diet, which would include a balanced portion of some fruit or a protein-rich vegetable, protein such as chicken and a high-fat portion that may be butter. The high-fat portion of this diet typically comes from the food-making ingredients; this may involve heavy cream, butter, or buttermilk, and creamy dressings such as ranch could also be mixed.

Unfortunately, with its potential for instantaneous results, this natural approach to healing had to give way to the new advancement of medicinal research.

Happily, again and perhaps for really good purposes, the ketogenic diet has made its way back into the spotlight!

You see, the cornerstone of the diet is to effectively stimulate the fat-burning processes of your own body to feel what the body wants for energy during the day. This implies that all the fat you consume and the accumulated fat in your body have both been fuel reserves that can be taped over by your body! No wonder that except among some persistent, hard to lose fat regions, this plan also helps you with weight reduction. It may be one of the explanations why you selected this eBook and looked into the ketogenic process, or you might have learned stories from your social group on how the keto diet really normalizes blood glucose levels and optimizes the cholesterol measurements and you are fascinated. Only by adopting this plan alone, how about the news of type 2 diabetes getting cured as well as stories of some diseases being prevented or tumors shrinking thanks to the beneficial impact of the keto diet? Even as a result of the diet, we do overlook the risk of heart disease!

All the above-mentioned advantages derive primarily from a single major mechanism in the ketogenic diet. The name of the game is ketosis.

In this very book, all information about the keto diet and intermittent fasting is provided and lets you know how it's helpful for quick and healthy weight loss.

# Chapter 1- Ketogenic Diet and Ketosis

You may be on a ketogenic diet or are contemplating it.

If you desire to kickstart with ketosis, then your ticket is for intermittent fasting.

Truth be known, it can be daunting to follow a ketogenic diet, mainly because there are too many things that you cannot consume. But be assured the truth-ketosis is spiritual.

Fortunately, whether you don't want to eat a ketogenic diet, you will easily get a route to ketosis.

When the body burns up ketones and fat for food instead of glucose, ketosis happens.

In two cases, that happens:

1.  there is no food coming (fasting) or

2. little or no carbohydrates come through (ketogenic dieting).

It regularly makes ketones in the process when your system is in the fat-burning phase; hence, you are in ketosis.

For the body to be in the process of ketosis is perfectly natural, and it was definitely a popular occurrence for humans across history that had intermittent accessibility to food and fasting times in between. For those following a Western diet, though, the physiological condition of ketosis is very unusual since we are all feeding. You basically get negligible ketones in your blood while you're consuming something else than a ketogenic diet. But it's very rare for our generation of people to be in a condition of ketosis unless you seek one out purposefully.

Post 8 hours of fasting, as you wake up, ketone levels are only starting to raise. Ketone output will speed up to provide more of the energy you need if you prolong your fast until noon, and your body will finally be in the renowned fat-burning condition of ketosis. If you want to manage to burn body fat at a high pace by keeping to your fast for 16 hours or a day or a few days, and not by consuming anything ketogenic, you need to live in ketosis!

A lot of focus is given to reaching ketosis through ketogenic diets, but if you consume keto foods, where do you suppose any of the ketones come from? And not the fat on the thighs and hips. Fasting for ketosis means that only the body fat comes from the ketones that feed the brain, thereby getting rid of it.

Ketosis is a condition in which the body creates compounds that are formed by the liver, labeled ketones. Crafted to supply organs and cells with nutrition, it may substitute sugar as an additional source of food. We get much of our energy from glucose in our conventional diet, rich in carbs which are processed from the carbohydrates that we consume throughout meals. Glucose is a fast energy supply, where insulin is needed as a kind of intermediary that tells the cells to open up and enables the flow of glucose so that it can be used as a mitochondrial fuel, better known as the fuel factories in our cells. The further sugars we eat, the more glucose is found in our blood, which suggests that the pancreas has to generate more insulin to promote the extraction of energy from usable blood sugar. In an organism where the metabolism is still natural, the cells readily embrace the insulin released by the pancreas, which then contributes to the effective use of blood glucose as energy. The concern is that our cells will actually become desensitized to insulin, contributing to a condition in which the pancreas is required to inject more and more insulin into the bloodstream only to clear the blood sugar levels and normalize them.

Insulin de-sensitivity or insulin tolerance is primarily induced by the constant enhanced presence of blood glucose and is typically caused by the intake of foods high in carbon. Picture of the cells of the body like a security guard at a bar, where you need to pay a charge to enter the club. Here, you play a glucose function, and the cost paid to join the club is insulin. If the club intensity is in accordance with the standard, the security officer doesn't really notice something odd and does not increase the admission fee needed. However, if you wake up clamoring to be allowed in just about every night, the bouncer understands the dire need and jacks up the insulin charge periodically in order to let glucose in. Gradually, at such a stage that the source of insulin, which in this situation is the pancreas, no longer generates any, the admission fee grows greater and greater. This is when the situation is diagnosed with type 2 diabetes, and the normal solution will include drugs or insulin injections for a lifetime. In the existence of glucose in the body system lies the crux of the matter here. Our blood sugar levels are raised every time we take in a carb-rich meal, which is not complicated in this day and age of fast food and sugary snacks, and insulin is enabled for the conversion into energy as well as the storage of the wasted waste into fat cells. This is where the normal furor begins, with condemnations pouring in as the cause of numerous ailments and dreaded weight gain with both glucose and insulin. It wouldn't be wrong if it claimed that insulin and glucose, as certain books have made them out to be, are most certainly not the source of all bad. To refer to our present diet as the leading cause of metabolic disorders and obesity plaguing the greater part of the developing world will be much more specific.

Link the ketogenic diet, which is where the shift toward the positive will be seen.

The keto diet, with a focus on being intentionally low carb, is a fat-based diet. This strategy is intended to decrease our consumption of sugar and starchy foods that are too easily affordable. Just a pleasant fact: in the old days, sugar was actually used as a preservative, and it's no accident that a number of the packaged goods we have now involve massive quantities of sugar so that it makes for longer shelf life. The hedonic appetite reaction in the brain has often been found to cause foods rich in sugar, ultimately allowing you to feed for the sake of gratification rather than actual hunger. Studies also found that sugar therapies are linked to the regions of the brain that are often responsible for opioid use and gambling. You know now that it appears like you can't resist tossing those caramelized sweets into the mouth.

So, we cut back on sugars, and this is where the fat comes in to offset the calories required to help the body. You will be looking at taking seventy-five percent of the daily calorie as fats on the regular ketogenic diet, approximately twenty percent as protein and the remaining five percent in the form of carbohydrates. We are doing it because, as we know, we want our key source of fuel to be fat. We will cause the body to induce ketosis only with the mixture of cutting down carbohydrates and growing our fat intake. We either do so with a diet that makes long-term, safe use, or we actually starve through ketosis. Yeah, sure, you heard it correctly; ketosis is the normal mechanism of the body that creates a shield against the lean periods where there is a lack of food.

## Chapter 2- Intermittent fasting and the ketogenic diet

In recent years, this has also been bandied about a lot, with some seeking to shed a misleading light on the keto diet by associating it with thirst.

To make it simpler, when our bodies feel that we do not have adequate glucose in the bloodstream, the ketosis mechanism is initiated. In order to ensure the continuous availability of nutrition for our cells and tissues, it then switches to our fat reserves to transform them into ketones via the liver. It does not mean that you are necessarily killing yourself on the keto diet! Any time someone says that, he got a little worked up.

How will a person who eats 1,800 to 2,000 calories on a regular basis, which is what you're going to get on the meal plan, starve effectively?

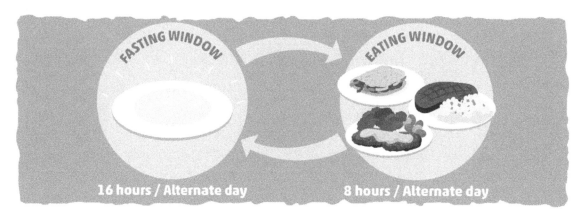

To be fair, during the hunter-gatherer days of our human past, ketosis comes in very handy. This was a time where agriculture wasn't that common, and what you searched or found relied on the food you consumed. This produced a scenario where there could be no calories for days at a time, so our bodies sent insulin to ferry it through our organs as glucose made its way through the environment, as well as hoarding the leftover glucose into fat cells for potential usage.

The body then reached the condition of ketosis by using the accumulated fats to provide nutrition during the lean periods when there was really little food to be found.

Our hunger hormones, like ghrelin, decrease their development during this stage, and the hormones that regulate satiety, like leptin, see their levels increased. All this is how our bodies want to make the most of it to make it easier for us to feel as comfortable as possible if nutritional supplies are scarce.

Today, quick forward to modern days, where food is practically only one or two streets away, or maybe just a car ride away, and we're not going to experience food scarcity like our predecessors in the Paleolithic. However, our bodies also retain the processes and pathways that have enabled them to function. That is the main explanation why we reduce carbohydrates and raise our regular fat consumption on the keto diet.

The condition of ketosis is triggered when we do so, and we get to reap all the biochemical advantages that the diet confers.

The fat we consume often goes into replenishing the body's fat reserves, which is why it won't be wrong to claim again when on the ketogenic diet, one should not starve!

# How the Intermitting Fasting Works

From the context of weight reduction, intermittent fasting operates by finding it more challenging to overeat during the day. A basic guideline such as "skip breakfast" or "eat only between 5 pm and 8 pm" will help keep you from reaching for sweets or consuming calorie-dense drinks that lead to weight gain during the day.

You'll also find it impossible to overeat, even though you work up a ferocious appetite when fasting. In fact, intermittent fasting appears to decrease the intake of daily energy and encourage fat loss.

This ensures that as long as you adhere to a shorter feeding time or a fixed number of meals, you can be willing to consume as much as you like and meet your objectives.

Your body may need to adapt itself to this new eating pattern when you first attempt intermittent fasting. Hunger pangs and strong cravings may strike you hard at first, but they will soon recede when your cells feast on accumulated fat and ketones.

Insulin removal, ketone synthesis and autophagy are the main pathways behind your ability to quickly lose weight and boost your health in the process. Our insulin levels drop incrementally as we accumulate time in a fasting condition. This facilitates the liberation of fat from our fat cells and activates the mechanism known as ketogenesis that generates ketones.

You'll reach a deeper state of ketosis as you continue your easy, become more successful at burning fat, and speed up the self-cleaning mechanism known as autophagy.

# Benefits of Intermitting Fasting

### 1. Enhanced regulation of blood sugar and resistance to insulin

This will also help boost blood sugar levels and improve one's cells' insulin response by allowing the body an occasional break from calorie intake. One research study showed that for six meals a day, intermittent fasting could also be a healthier option than having the same calorie deficit.

The two dietary strategies can function synergistically to boost blood sugar regulation when paired with the keto diet, which has also been shown to assist with insulin tolerance and type 2 diabetes. More study on the results of using them in tandem, however, is needed.

## 2. Psychic Clarity

Your brain will essentially operate on ketones, which are extracted through fat dissolution in the liver until the body is keto-adapted.

Fat is thought to be one of the body's most energy-efficient resources to work on, and your mind is a major energy user.

When you do not regularly refill on grains and fruits, most high-carb supporters fight for the malnutrition your body endures. They expect you to take a granola bar and an apple around you everywhere you go, but the advantage of Keto is that you don't.

And if the body is full of glycogen (which is more definitely if you are in ketosis), the excess of fat from the meals you consume and shop you have will depend on it. That ensures that your brain powerhouse will operate at maximum capacity all the time. Less emotional fogginess and more attention.

You can begin to lose fat automatically when you get used to dieting. In other terms, feed only when you are starving. Don't arrange the fasting; let it arise spontaneously.

## 3. Fitness

People still claim that if you don't use the benefit of pre-and post-exercise meals while you work out, you're going to lose muscle.

This is not inherently real, and when you're adapted to ketosis, it is much less so.

In the long run, fasting while practicing can contribute to a variety of advantages, including:

1.  **Greater mutation adaptations** - Studies indicate that when you work out in a fasting condition, your training efficiency will improve in the long run.

2.  **Enhanced muscle synthesis**- Experiments indicate that when you exercise in a fasting condition and use sufficient nutrient consumption, muscle gains are improved.

3.  **Increased reaction to post-workout meals**-Studies suggests that the accelerated ingestion of nutrients after a short exercise will contribute to better outcomes.

# Mechanism Behind the Benefits

Intermittent fasting is so effective that it can be used to reduce calories, trigger ketosis, and enable the mechanisms of autophagy induced by protein restriction and hunger.

This is what happens to our cells as we consume three or more meals a day, which meets our normal calorie requirements fully. Your cells will also be backed up with non-essential proteins and poisonous chemicals, sometimes after consuming the healthiest diets, but what can you do?

You soon, not from cooking, but from being consumed by other commitments, to ensure you clean your real bedroom. You need to fast with food to ensure sure the cells will clean themselves.

Not only can this fasting phase trigger this cleanup for your cells, but it will increase the output of your ketones and facilitate fat burning as well. Simply stated, by incorporating intermittent fasting into the keto diet, coupled with the consequences of autophagy, you can enjoy the advantages of Keto more easily.

In addition, you will raise ketone amounts, lose more fat, and improve autophagy more than you can with intermittent fasting alone if you begin to implement intermittent fasting and exercise together.

Overall, the evidence for intermittent fasting shows that it will be a perfect complement to the keto lifestyle for certain persons, whether you include activity or not. Before you start, though, it is important to be acquainted with the unpleasant signs that can occur.

# Chapter 3- How autophagy and ketosis are synergic?

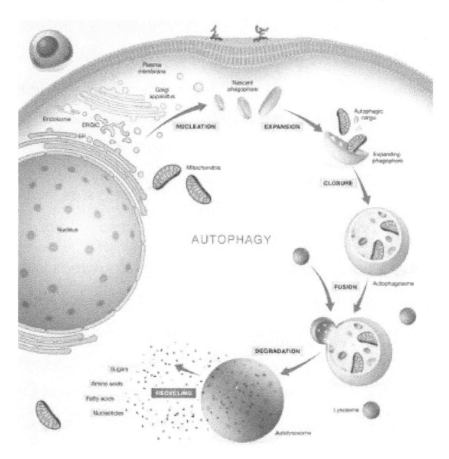

In order to reconstruct healthy, healthier cells, autophagy is the body's method of wiping out dead cells.

Auto" implies self, and "phagy" implies eating." So, 'self-eating' is the literal sense of autophagy.

That is often referred to as "self-devouring." Although it might seem like something you would wish to occur to your body, your ultimate wellbeing is actually advantageous.

It is since autophagy is an evolved method of self-preservation by which the organism can extract and regenerate sections of dysfunctional cells for cellular repair and hygiene.

The aim of autophagy is to eliminate debris and return to optimum smooth operation through self-regulation.

Around the same moment, it's recycling and washing, almost like touching the body on a reset button. Plus, as a reaction to different stressors and contaminants accumulated in our bodies, it encourages resilience and adaptation.

Note that autophagy simply means "self-eating." Therefore, it makes sense that it is understood that intermittent fasting and ketogenic diets induce autophagy.

The most successful method to cause autophagy is by fasting.

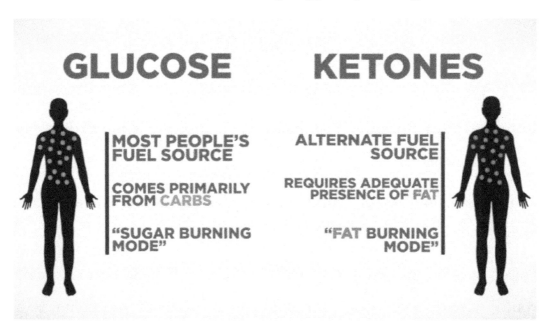

Ketosis, a high-fat and low-carb diet, offers the same advantages to eating without fasting, such as a shortcut that causes the same advantageous biochemical adjustments. It allows the body a break to concentrate on its own wellbeing and repair by not stressing the body with an external load.

You receive about 75 percent of the recommended daily calories from fat in the keto diet and 5 to 10 percent of your calories from carbohydrates.

This alteration in calorie sources allows the biochemical processes in the body to change. Instead of the glucose that is extracted from carbohydrates, it would start using fat for food.

In reaction to this ban, the body will begin to start creating ketone bodies that have several protective effects. Khorana says studies show that ketosis, which has neuroprotective functions, may also cause starvation-induced autophagy.

In all diets, low glucose levels exist and are related to low insulin and high levels of glucagon. And the degree of glucagon is the one that initiates autophagy.

It brings the constructive stress that wakes up the survival repair mode when the body is low on sugar by fasting or ketosis.

Exercise is one non-diet region that can also play a part in causing autophagy. Physical activity can, according to one animal research, cause autophagy in organs that are part of the processes of metabolic control.

# Chapter 4- Keto Diet and weight loss

When we start on a ketogenic diet, one of the first items we still lose is most certainly water weight. As adipose fats, the body stores glucose, although there is a limited supply of glucose that is processed as glycogen, composed mainly of water. Glycogen is intended to provide rapid bursting capacity, the kind we use when we run or raise weights. The body switches to glycogen as the first source of energy supply as we cut carbohydrates, which is why water weight is lost in the initial phases. This initial blast of weight reduction may be a morale booster for everyone, and for people who conform to the keto diet, it is a positive signpost for what is to come. Water weight is readily lost and gained, as a side note. This suggests that even those who first see certain outcomes in the keto diet and then wish to get off the track for some reason, as carbohydrates become the daily calorie mainstay, the odds are their weight would swell back up.

For the rest that conforms to the ketogenic diet, what comes next will be the fat burning process of the body that is responsible for the impressive effects of weight loss shown by many. The underlying principle is also the same in that adipose fats are still activated by the organs and cells of the body as energy sources, contributing to a normal state of depletion of fat and thus accompanying reducing weight.

The burning of fat is not the sole explanation that the keto diet demonstrates weight reduction.

Hunger reduction and improvement of pleasure during meals are also explanations that people are better able to lose weight whilst on a diet. One of the long-standing ideals of weight management has always been the adage of drinking less and doing more. The entire premise is to establish a calorie shortage in such a way that the body is forced to depend on its stored energy reserves to make up for the requisite expenditure. That seems quick and straightforward on paper, but it may be as challenging as scaling Mount Everest for someone who has been through scenarios where you have had to deliberately curtail your food on a hungry stomach!

Through the ketogenic diet, thanks to the modification of the hormones that regulate sensations of appetite and fullness, you realize that you will have normal hunger suppression. In addition, the food we usually eat while on a diet often assists with weight reduction. It is understood that fats and protein are more relaxing and rewarding than sugary carbs. We do two items almost concurrently as we turn to a high-fat diet when cutting back on the carbohydrates. Only because we feel like it, not because we are very hungry, easing back on carbohydrates, particularly the sugar stuff, reduces the urge to consume. Charging high the consumption of fat often causes the satiety impact even easier and helps you to feel complete. This is part of so many keto dieters claim that without having the smallest pinch of hunger, they will go for two and a half or even two meals a day.

We account for a regular caloric consumption that varies from 1,800 to 2,000 calories on our keto meal schedule, but we do not even use calorie limits to minimize weight. The truth is that those tiny and harmless-looking snacks that fill the period between dinners will not appear much in your life when you feel fullness and enjoyment from your meals! Think about it: the usual go-to sweets, donuts, candy, and cookies, are left out purely, so you are less inclined to give in to hedonistic appetite induced mainly by the same sugar treats in reducing extra calories which would have otherwise been converted to adipose fat tissue, that goes a very long way.

To sum up, without the usual calorie limit in most weight reduction diets, the ketogenic diet provides for meals. It also offers a supporting hand in the production of symptoms of hunger suppression such that you do not have to struggle with those treacherous hunger pangs! The lack of carb munchies is also present, which may theoretically disrupt any diet. With as minimal disturbance to our everyday life as possible, this helps one to experience normal weight loss. There is no need to deploy calorie counters, no need for a problematic six to eight meals a day, and certainly no strange or amusing workout exercises required. If you pair it with the satisfying high-fat keto meals, you enter a scenario where hunger could indeed become an outsider.

As another good spin-off, having to re-learn what real hunger feels like still arrives. We get incidents of hunger on a carb-rich diet, and our blood sugar levels appear to fluctuate dramatically as our cells become increasingly desensitized by insulin. The propensity to feed on impulse is often enhanced by sugar, which can really ruin any diet! We will also have to wake up and take care anytime we feel those hunger pangs when we cut back on carbohydrates and ratchet up on the fats, so that will be proper signs that the body needs extra energy.

## Chapter 5- Benefits of Ketogenic Diet

All in all, the straightforward method to the keto diet has inspired individuals to engage with it, resulting in many variants of the keto diet that are available. The keto diet method has been one of the most attempted regimes, and in the last few years, it has grown tremendously in prominence.

Although the key advantage of Keto is successful weight loss, metabolic boosting and hunger control, such advantages include the following-

1. Acne may be decreased by the keto diet since glucose restriction can tip the dynamics of bacteria in the intestine that influences the face.

2. It is known to deter and cure some cancers and, in addition to radiation and chemotherapy, is seen as a supportive medication since it allows cancer cells to undergo additional oxidative stress, allowing them to die.

3. This diet provides your body with a better and healthy source of energy and thus will make you feel more energetic throughout the day.

4. A reduction in cholesterol is caused by keto diets, and the presence of healthy cholesterol is improved.

5. The brain and nerve cells are reinforced and preserved. In addition, it is understood to manage diseases such as Alzheimer's, Parkinson's etc.

6. Many types of research have shown that the keto diet helps to lower down the low-density lipoproteins or the bad cholesterol over time and have been shown to eliminate diseases such as type 2 diabetes.

7. It aids in losing weight as the body burns down the fat as the prior energy source, and one will primarily be using the fat stored in the body as an energy source while in a fasting mode.

8. A Keto diet has been shown to improve cholesterol levels and triglyceride levels most associated with arterial buildup.

9. Known for managing epilepsy-like disorders, Ovarian polycystic disease, etc.

10. The ketogenic diet promises many keto advantages, but a true effort is to initiate the keto diet. It is a restrictive diet that seeks to reduce one's carb consumption to about 50 grams a day, so visiting a dietician to work out and modify the diet according to one's needs is advantageous.

# Chapter 6- The 15-day Meal Plan with Low-Carb Recipes that fit the Intermittent Fasting Diet

Eating Keto involves limiting the net carb consumption such that energy and ketones are generated by your body metabolizing fat. For many, this means reducing net carbs to 20 grams a day.

The keto diet could be perfect for you if you are trying to optimize advantages such as curing type 2 diabetes or if you want to lose the extra kilos

A more balanced low-carb diet could be a safer option for you if you want more carbohydrates in your diet and if you don't have type 2 diabetes or have a lot of weight to lose. It may be better to adopt mild low carb, but it may also be less successful than Keto, suggesting you may get more modest outcomes.

**Day 1**

Breakfast- Scrambled eggs

Lunch-Bacon and Zucchini Noodles Salad

Dinner- Spinach Soup

## Day 2

Breakfast- Keto Frittata

Lunch-Keto Roasted Pepper and Cauliflower

Dinner-Buffalo Blue Cheese Chicken Wedges

## Day 3

Breakfast- Breakfast Bowl

Lunch-Lunch Tacos

Dinner-Lemon Dill Trout

## Day 4

Breakfast- Poached Eggs

Lunch-Simple Pizza Rolls

Dinner-Special Fish Pie

## Day 5

Breakfast- Bright Morning Smoothie

Lunch-Lunch Stuffed Peppers

Dinner-Cauliflower Bread Garlic Sticks

## Day 6

Breakfast-Pumpkin Muffins

Lunch-Lunch Stuffed Peppers

Dinner- Buffalo Blue Cheese Chicken Wedges

## Day 7

Breakfast- Keto Breakfast Mix

Lunch-Lunch Caesar Salad

Dinner-Sage N Orange Breast of Duck

## Day 8

Breakfast-Pumpkin Pie Spiced Latte

Lunch-Keto Roasted Pepper and Cauliflower

Dinner- Salmon with Caper Sauce

## Day 9

Breakfast- Strawberry Protein Smoothie

Lunch-Keto Slow Cooker Buffalo Chicken Soup

Dinner-Cauliflower Bread Garlic Sticks

## Day 10

Breakfast-Delicious Eggs and Sausages

Lunch-Special Lunch Burgers

Dinner-Tossed Brussel Sprout Salad

## Day 11

Breakfast-Bright Morning Smoothie

Lunch-Keto Lunch Jambalaya

Dinner- Spinach Soup

## Day 12

Breakfast-Keto Frittata

Lunch-Lunch Tacos

Dinner-Special Fish Pie

## Day 13

Breakfast-Feta and Asparagus Delight

Lunch-Keta Chicken Enchilada Soup

Dinner-Bok Choy Stir Fry

## Day 14

Breakfast-Scrambled Eggs

Lunch- Simple Pizza Rolls

Dinner- Lemon Dill Trout

## Day 15

Breakfast-Strawberry Protein Smoothie

Lunch-Bacon and Zucchini Noodles Salad

Dinner-Spinach Soup

The list of food items in this meal plan is not exhaustive. You can change the menu as per the availability of the products.

If you wish to avoid your breakfast or any other meal in order to practice fasting, then you are supposed to keep drinking water in that period of time and also make sure that you take multi-vitamins prescribed by a physician.

Following provided is a list of foods that you can take while on intermittent fasting inspired keto diet-

1. Vegetables
2. Proteins
3. Oil and good fats
4. Beverages
5. Seeds and nuts
6. Diary

The list of foods provided under are to be completely avoided or should be taken in a minimal amount-

1. Processed Foods
2. Artificial Sweeteners
3. Alcohol
4. Milk
5. Refined fats
6. Legumes
7. Soy Products
8. Grains

# Chapter 7- Breakfast Recipes

## 7.1 Delicious Poached Eggs

Ready in about 45 minutes | Servings-4 | Difficulty- Easy

### Ingredients

- Three minced garlic cloves
- One tablespoon of ghee
- One chopped white onion
- One chopped Serrano pepper
- Salt and black pepper to the taste
- One chopped red bell pepper

- Three chopped tomatoes

- One teaspoon of paprika

- One teaspoon of cumin

- A quarter teaspoon of chili powder

- One tablespoon of chopped cilantro

- Six eggs

**Instructions**

1. Heat the pan over medium heat with the ghee, add the onion, stir and cook and stir for ten minutes.

2. Add the garlic and Serrano pepper, stir and cook over medium heat for a minute.

3. Add red bell pepper and cook for 10 minutes, stirring and cooking.

4. Add the tomatoes, pepper, salt, chili powder, paprika and cumin, stir and cook for 10 minutes.

5. In the pan, crack the eggs, season them with pepper and salt, cover the pan and cook for another 6 minutes.

6. In the end, sprinkle with cilantro and serve.

## 7.2 Delicious Eggs and Sausages

Ready in about 45 minutes | Servings-6 | Difficulty- Easy

**Ingredient**

- Five tablespoons of ghee

- Twelve eggs

- Salt and black pepper as per taste

- One of torn spinach
- Twelve slices of ham
- Two chopped sausages
- One chopped yellow onion
- One chopped red bell pepper

**Instructions**

1. Heat a saucepan over medium heat with one tablespoon of ghee, add the onion and sausages, stir and cook for five minutes.
2. Add the bell pepper, pepper and salt, stir and cook for an additional three minutes and place in a bowl.
3. Melt and divide the rest of the ghee into 1two cups of cake molds.
4. In each cupcake mold, add a slice of ham, divide each spinach and then the sausage mix.
5. Break an egg on top, place everything in the oven and bake for 20 minutes at 425 ° Fahrenheit
6. Before serving, leave your cupcakes to cool down a bit.

## 7.3 Delicious Breakfast Bowl
Ready in about 30 minutes | Servings-1 | Difficulty- Easy

**Ingredients**

- Four ounces of ground beef
- One chopped yellow onion
- Eight sliced mushrooms
- Salt and black pepper as per taste
- Two whisked eggs

- One tablespoon of coconut oil

- Half a teaspoon of teaspoon smoked paprika

- One avocado, pitted, peeled and chopped

- Twelve pitted and sliced black olives

## Instructions

1. Heat a saucepan over medium heat with the coconut oil, add the onions, mushrooms, pepper and salt, stir and cook for five minutes.

2. Add the beef and paprika, stir, cook and transfer to a bowl for 10 minutes.

3. Over medium heat, heat the pan again, add the eggs, some pepper and salt and scramble.

4. Put the beef mix back in the pan and stir.

5. Add the olives and avocado, stir, and cook over medium heat for a minute

6. Transfer and serve in a bowl.

## 7.4 Keto Breakfast Mix

Ready in about 20 minutes | Servings-2 | Difficulty- Easy

## Ingredients

- Five tablespoons of unsweetened coconut flakes

- Seven tablespoons of Hemp seeds

- Five tablespoons of Ground Flaxseed

- Two tablespoons of ground Sesame

- Two tablespoons of unsweetened cocoa, dark

- Two tablespoons of Psyllium husk

## Instructions:

1. Grind the sesame and the flaxseed. Ensure that you only grind the sesame seeds for a short time.

2. In a jar, mix all the ingredients and shake them well.

3. Keep refrigerated until ready for consumption.

4. Serve softened with black coffee or still water and, if you want to increase your fat intake, add coconut oil. It also combines well with cream or with cheese from mascarpone.

## 7.5 Pumpkin Pie Keto Spiced Latte

Ready in about 20 minutes | Servings-2 | Difficulty- Easy

### Ingredients

- Two cups of strong and freshly brewed coffee
- One cup of Coconut Milk
- A quarter cup of Pumpkin Puree
- Half teaspoon of Cinnamon
- One teaspoon of Vanilla Extract
- Two teaspoons of Pumpkin Pie Spice Blend
- 15 drops of Liquid Stevia
- Two tablespoons of Butter
- Two tablespoons of Heavy Whipping Cream

### Instructions

1. Cook the pumpkin, butter, milk and spices over medium-low flame,

2. Add two cups of solid coffee and blend together until bubbling.

3. Remove from the stove, apply cream and stevia, and then whisk together with an electric mixer.

4. Top with whipped cream and enjoy.

## 7.6 Keto Frittata

Ready in about one hour 10 minutes | Servings-4 | Difficulty- Moderate

### Ingredients

- Nine ounces of spinach
- Twelve eggs
- One ounce of pepperoni
- One teaspoon of minced garlic
- Salt and black pepper to the taste
- Five ounces of shredded mozzarella
- Half cup of grated parmesan
- Half cup of ricotta cheese
- Four tablespoons of olive oil
- A pinch of nutmeg

### Instructions

1. Squeeze out the spinach liquid and put it in a bowl.
2. Mix the eggs with the salt, nutmeg, pepper, and garlic in another bowl and whisk well.
3. Add the spinach, ricotta and parmesan and whisk well.
4. Pour this into a saucepan, sprinkle on top with mozzarella and pepperoni, place in the oven and bake for 45 minutes at 375 ° Fahrenheit.
5. Leave the frittata for a few minutes to cool down before serving.

## 7.7 Keto Fall Pumpkin Spiced French Toast

Ready in about 20 minutes | Servings-2 | Difficulty- Easy

## Ingredients

- Four slices of Pumpkin Bread
- One large Egg
- Two tablespoons of cream
- Half teaspoon of Vanilla Extract
- 1/8 teaspoon of Orange Extract
- A quarter teaspoon of Pumpkin Pie Spice
- Two tablespoons of butter

## Instructions

Cook the pumpkin, butter, milk and spices over a medium-low flame.

Add two cups of solid coffee and blend together until bubbling.

Remove from the stove, apply cream and stevia, and then whisk together with an electric mixer.

Top with whipped cream and serve.

## 7.8 Scrambled Eggs

Ready in about 20 minutes | Servings-1 | Difficulty- Easy

## Ingredients

- Four chopped bell mushrooms
- Three whisked eggs
- Salt and black pepper to the taste
- Two chopped ham slices
- A quarter cup of chopped red bell pepper
- Half cup of chopped spinach

- One tablespoon of coconut oil

**Instructions**

Heat a saucepan over medium heat with half the oil, add the mushrooms, spinach, bell pepper and ham, stir and simmer for four minutes.

Heat up another pan over medium heat with the rest of the oil, add the eggs and scramble them.

Stir in the vegetables and ham, pepper and salt, stir, simmer and cook for one minute and then serve.

## 7.9 Feta and Asparagus Delight

Ready in about 35 minutes | Servings-2 | Difficulty- Easy

**Ingredients**

- Twelve asparagus spears
- One tablespoon of olive oil
- Two chopped green onions
- One minced garlic clove
- Six eggs
- Salt and black pepper to the taste
- Half cup of feta cheese

**Instructions**

1. Heat a pan over medium heat with some water, add asparagus, stir for eight minutes, drain well, chop two spears and reserve the remainder.

2. Over medium heat, heat a pan with the oil, add the garlic, onions and chopped asparagus, stir and cook for five minutes.

3. Add salt, pepper and eggs, stir, cover and cook for five minutes.

4. On top of your frittata, arrange the whole asparagus, sprinkle with cheese, place in the oven at 350 ° F and bake for nine minutes.

5. Divide and serve between plates.

## 7.10 Eggs Baked in Avocados

Ready in about 30 minutes | Servings-4 | Difficulty- Easy

### Ingredients

- Two avocados, cut in halves and pitted
- Four eggs
- Salt and black pepper to the taste
- One tablespoon of chopped chives

### Instructions

1. Scoop some of the avocado halves with some flesh and assemble them in a baking dish.

2. In each avocado, crack an egg, season with pepper and salt, place them at 425 degrees F in the oven and bake for 20 minutes.

3. In the end, sprinkle the chives and serve them for breakfast.

# Chapter 8- Lunch Recipes

## 8.1 Lunch Caesar Salad

Ready in about 10 minutes | Servings-2 | Difficulty- Easy

### Ingredients

- One pitted, peeled and sliced avocado

- Salt and black pepper to the taste

- Three tablespoons of creamy Caesar dressing

- One cup of cooked and crumbled bacon

- One grilled and shredded chicken breast

### Instructions

1. Mix the avocado with the chicken breast and bacon in a salad bowl and stir.

2. Add salt and pepper, Caesar dressing, toss to coat, split into two bowls and serve.

## 8.2 Keto Lunch Jambalaya

Ready in about 40 minutes | Servings-2 | Difficulty- Moderate

### Ingredients

- One medium cauliflower
- One coarsely chopped green pepper
- Two stalks of coarsely chopped celery
- One diced small onion
- Two minced cloves of garlic
- Three cubed boneless chicken breasts
- Eight ounces of sliced smoked sausage
- Eight ounces of ham, cubed
- Fourteen and a half ounce can of diced tomatoes, undrained
- Eight ounce can of tomato sauce
- Three teaspoons of Cajun Seasoning
- Salt and pepper according to taste
- Cooking oil

### Instructions

1. Heat two tablespoons of oil in an 8-quart Dutch oven or skillet.
2. On a medium-high flame, sauté the peppers, garlic, chicken, celery, onion and Cajun seasoning until the chicken is almost cooked.
3. Add the cauliflower, ham and sausage. Mix thoroughly.
4. Add the tomato sauce and tomatoes to the mix. Bring it to a simmer, and then turn it back to low.

5. Cover until the cauliflower is moist but not mushy, and cook for around twenty minutes.

6. Season with salt and pepper and then serve after removing from heat.

## 8.3 Lunch Tacos

Ready in about 40 minutes | Servings-3 | Difficulty- Moderate

**Ingredients**

- Two cups of grated cheddar cheese
- One small pitted, peeled and chopped avocado
- One cup of cooked favorite taco meat
- Two teaspoons of sriracha sauce
- A quarter cup of chopped tomatoes
- Cooking spray
- Salt and black pepper as per taste

**Instructions**

1. Spray on a lined baking dish with some cooking oil.

2. Cover on the baking sheet with cheddar cheese, put in the oven at 400 degrees F, and bake for 15 minutes.

3. Spread the taco meat over the cheese and cook for a further 10 minutes.

4. Meanwhile, combine the avocado with tomatoes, sriracha, salt and pepper in a bowl and swirl.

5. Spread this over the layers of taco and cheddar, let the tacos cool down a little, use a pizza slicer to slice and serve for lunch.

## 8.4 Keto Chicken Enchilada Soup

Ready in about 40 minutes | Servings-3 | Difficulty- Moderate

## Ingredients

- Six oz. Shredded chicken
- Two teaspoons of Cumin
- One teaspoon of Oregano
- One teaspoon of Chili Powder
- Half teaspoon of Cayenne Pepper
- Half cup of chopped cilantro
- Half medium Lime, juiced
- three tablespoons of Olive Oil
- Three stalks of diced Celery
- One medium diced Red Bell Pepper, diced
- Two teaspoons of garlic, minced
- Four cups of Chicken Broth
- One cup of Diced Tomatoes
- Eight oz. of Cream Cheese

## Instructions

1. Heat the oil in a pan and add the celery and pepper. Add the tomatoes and cook for 2-3 minutes once the celery is soft.
2. Add the spices to the pan and mix well.
3. Add the chicken broth and the cilantro to the mixture, boil, and then reduce to low for 20 minutes to simmer.
4. Then add the cream cheese and bring it back to the boil. Once it has cooked, reduce the heat to low and cover and cook for 25 minutes.
5. Scrap the chicken and add it to the pot, then top it with half the lime juice.

6. Mix together everything.

7. Serve with coriander, sour cream or shredded cheese.

## 8.5 Simple Pizza Rolls

Ready in about 40 minutes | Servings-6 | Difficulty- Moderate

**Ingredients**

- A quarter cups of chopped mixed red and green bell peppers

- Two cups of shredded mozzarella cheese

- One teaspoon of pizza seasoning

- Two tablespoons of chopped onion

- One chopped tomato

- Salt and black pepper to the taste

- A quarter cups of pizza sauce

- Half cup of crumbled and cooked sausage

**Instructions**

1. On a lined and lightly oiled baking dish, spread mozzarella cheese, sprinkle pizza seasoning on top, put at 400 °F in the oven and bake for 20 minutes.

2. Spread the sausage, onion, tomatoes and bell pepper all over and drizzle the tomato sauce at the top. Taking the pizza crust out of the oven.

3. Place them back in the oven and bake for ten more minutes.

4. Take the pizza from the oven, leave it aside for a few minutes, break it into six pieces, roll each slice and eat it for lunch.

## 8.6 Lunch Stuffed Peppers

Ready in about 50 minutes | Servings-4 | Difficulty- Moderate

**Ingredients**

- Four big banana peppers cut into halves lengthwise

- One tablespoon of ghee

- Salt and black pepper to the taste

- Half teaspoon of herbs de Provence

- One pound of chopped sweet sausage

- Three tablespoons of chopped yellow onions

- Some marinara sauce

- A drizzle of olive oil

## Instructions

1. Season the banana peppers with pepper and salt, drizzle with the oil, rub well and bake for 20 minutes in the oven at 325 ° F.

2. Meanwhile, over medium, prepare, heat a skillet, add the pieces of sausage, mix and cook for 5 minutes.

3. Combine the onion, herbs, salt, pepper and ghee, mix well and simmer for 5 minutes.

4. Take the peppers out of the oven, load them with the sausage mix, place them in a dish that is oven-proof, drizzle them with the marinara sauce, placed them back in the oven and bake for another 10 minutes.

5. Serve and enjoy.

## 8.7 Special Lunch Burgers

Ready in about 35 minutes | Servings-8 | Difficulty- Moderate

## Ingredients

- One pound ground brisket

- One pound ground beef

KETO BREAD COOKBOOK FOR FAMILY BY ALESSANDRO VASQUEZ

- Salt and black pepper as per taste

- Eight butter slices

- One tablespoon of minced garlic

- One tablespoon of Italian seasoning

- Two tablespoons of mayonnaise

- One tablespoon of ghee

- Two tablespoons of olive oil

- One chopped yellow onion

- One tablespoon of water

**Instructions**

1. Mix the beef, pepper, salt, Italian herbs, mayo and garlic with the brisket in a bowl and stir well.

2. Form 8 patties into each one to create a pocket.

3. With butter-slices, stuff each burger and seal it.

4. Over medium pressure, heat the pan with the oil, add the onions, stir and simmer for 2 minutes.

5. Apply the water, swirl and pick them up in the pan corner.

6. Put the burgers with the onions in the pan and cook them for ten minutes over moderate flame.

7. Flip them over, apply the ghee, and simmer for ten more minutes.

8. Break the burgers into buns and place them on top of caramelized onions.

## 8.8 Keto Roasted Pepper and Cauliflower

Ready in about 50 minutes | Servings-4 | Difficulty- Moderate

**Ingredients**

- Two halved and de-seeded Red Bell Peppers

- Half head of cauliflower cut into florets

- Two tablespoons of Duck Fat

- Three medium diced green Onions

- Three cups of Chicken Broth

- Half cup Heavy Cream

- Four tablespoons of Duck Fat

- Salt and pepper as per taste

- One teaspoon of Garlic Powder

- One teaspoon of Dried Thyme

- One teaspoon of Smoked Paprika

- A quarter teaspoon of Red Pepper Flakes

- Four oz. Goat Cheese

## Instructions

1. Preheat the oven to 400 °F

Clean, de-seed, and half-slice the peppers

Broil until the flesh is burnt and blackened for about 10-15 minutes.

Place in a container with a cover to steam when finished cooking cauliflower.

Sprinkle two tablespoons of melted duck fat, pepper and salt into sliced cauliflower florets.

Cook for 30-35 minutes in the oven.

Pick off the skins of the peppers by gently peeling them off.

Heat Four tablespoons of duck fat in a pot and add the diced green onion.

To toast, apply seasonings to the plate, then add red pepper, chicken broth, and cauliflower to the skillet.

For 10-20 minutes, let this boil.

Bring the mixture to an immersion blender. Make sure that it emulsifies both fats.

Then apply the cream and combine.

Serve with some bacon and goats' cheese. Add thyme and green onion to garnish.

## 8.9 Bacon and Zucchini Noodles Salad

Ready in about 10 minutes | Servings-2 | Difficulty- Easy

### Ingredients

- One cup of baby spinach
- Four cups of zucchini noodles
- 1/3 cups of crumbled bleu cheese
- 1/3 cups of thick cheese dressing
- Half cup of cooked and crumbled bacon
- Black pepper as per taste

### Instructions

1. Mix the spinach with the bacon, zucchini noodles and the bleu cheese in a salad dish, and toss.
2. Apply the black pepper and cheese dressing as per taste, toss well to cover, distribute into two bowls and eat.

## 8.10 Keto Slow Cooker Buffalo Chicken Soup

Ready in about 6 hours and 20 minutes | Servings-2 | Difficulty- Hard

### Ingredients

- Three Chicken Thighs, de-boned and sliced

- One teaspoon of Onion Powder

- One teaspoon of Garlic Powder

- Half teaspoon Celery Seed

- A quarter cup of butter

- Half cup of Frank's Hot Sauce

- Three cups of Beef Broth

- One cup of Heavy Cream

- Two oz. Cream Cheese

- A quarter teaspoon of Xanthan Gum

- Salt and pepper as per taste

## Instructions

1. Begin by de-boning the chicken thighs, break the chicken into chunks and place the remainder of the ingredients in a slow cooker in the crockpot with the exception of cream, cheese, and xanthan gum.

2. Set a low, slow cooker for 6 hours (or a high one for 3 hours) and cook fully.

3. Remove the chicken from the slow cooker until it is done, and shred it with a fork.

4. Using the slow cooker to combine cream, cheese, and xanthan gum. Combine it all together

5. Transfer the chicken to the slow cooker and blend.

6. Season it with salt, pepper, and hot sauce. Serve.

# Chapter 9- Dinner Recipes

## 9.1 Buffalo Blue Cheese Chicken Wedges

Ready in about 40 minutes | Servings-2 | Difficulty-Moderate

### Ingredients

- One head of lettuce

- Bleu cheese dressing

- Two tablespoons of crumbled blue cheese

- Four strips of bacon

- Two boneless chicken breasts

- 3/4 cup of any buffalo sauce

### Instructions

1. Boil a big pot of salted water.

2. Add two chicken breasts to the water and simmer for 30 minutes, or until the internal temperature of the chicken reaches 180 °C.

3. Let the chicken rest for 10 minutes to cool.

4. Take apart the chicken into strips using a fork.

5. Cook and cool bacon strips, crumble reserve,

6. Merge the scrapped chicken and buffalo sauce over medium heat, then mix until warm.

7. Break the lettuce into wedges and apply the appropriate amount of blue cheese dressing to it.

8. Add crumbles of blue cheese.

9. Add the chicken-pulled buffalo.

10. Cover with more crumbles of blue cheese and fried crumbled bacon.

11. Serve.

## 9.2 Cauliflower Bread Garlic sticks

Ready in about 55 minutes | Servings-2 | Difficulty-Moderate

### Ingredients

- Two cups of cauliflower rice
- One tablespoon of organic butter
- Three teaspoons of minced garlic
- A quarter teaspoon of red pepper flakes
- Half teaspoon of Italian seasoning
- 1/8 teaspoon of kosher salt
- One cup of shredded mozzarella cheese
- One egg
- One cup of grated parmesan cheese

### Instructions

1. Preheat the oven to 350° F.

2. Sauté the red pepper flakes and garlic for nearly three minutes and transfer to a bowl of cooked cauliflower. Melt the butter in a small skillet over low heat.

3. Mix the Italian seasoning and salt together.

4. Afterward, refrigerate for 10 minutes.

5. Add the mozzarella cheese and egg to the cauliflower mixture until slightly cooled.

6. A creamy paste in a thin layer lined with parchment paper on a thinly oiled 9-9 baking dish.

7. Bake for thirty minutes.

8. Remove from the oven and finish with a little more parmesan and mozzarella cheese.

9. Put them back in the oven and cook for an extra 8 minutes.

10. Remove from the oven and slice into sticks of the appropriate duration.

## 9.3 Tasty Baked Fish

Ready in about 40 minutes | Servings-4 | Difficulty-Moderate

**Ingredients**

- One pound of haddock
- Three teaspoons of water
- Two tablespoons of lemon juice
- Salt and black pepper as per taste
- Two tablespoons of mayonnaise
- One teaspoon of dill weed
- Cooking spray
- A pinch of old bay seasoning

## Instructions

1. With some cooking oil, spray a baking dish.

2. Apply the lemon juice, fish and water and toss to cover a little bit.

3. Apply salt, pepper, seasoning with old bay and dill weed and mix again.

4. Add mayonnaise and spread evenly.

5. Place it at 350 ° F in the oven and bake for thirty minutes.

6. Split and serve on a plate.

## 9.4 Spinach Soup

Ready in about 25 minutes | Servings-8 | Difficulty-Easy

## Ingredients

- Two tablespoons of ghee

- Twenty ounces of chopped spinach

- One teaspoon of minced garlic

- Salt and black pepper as per taste

- Forty-five ounces of chicken stock

- Half teaspoons of nutmeg, ground

- Two cups of heavy cream

- One chopped yellow onion

## Instructions

1. Heat a pot over medium heat with the ghee, add the onion, stir and simmer for 4 minutes.

2. Stir in the garlic, stir and simmer for a minute.

3. Add spinach and stock and simmer for 5 minutes.

4. Blend the broth with an immersion mixer and reheat the soup.

5. Stir in pepper, nutmeg, salt, and cream, stir and simmer for a further 5 minutes.

6. Ladle it into cups and serve.

## 9.5 Tossed Brussel Sprout Salad

Ready in about 30 minutes | Servings-2 | Difficulty-Easy

### Ingredients

- Six Brussels sprouts

- Half teaspoon of apple cider vinegar

- One teaspoon of olive/grapeseed oil

- A quarter teaspoon of salt

- A quarter teaspoon of pepper

- One tablespoon of freshly grated parmesan

### Instructions

1. Break and clean Brussels sprouts in half lengthwise, root on, then cut thin slices through them in the opposite direction.

2. Cut the roots and remove them until chopped.

3. Toss the apple cider, oil, pepper and salt together.

4. Sprinkle, blend and eat with your parmesan cheese.

## 9.6 Special Fish Pie

Ready in about One hour 20 minutes | Servings-6 | Difficulty-Moderate

### Ingredients

- One chopped red onion

- Two skinless and medium sliced salmon fillets

- Two skinless and medium sliced mackerel fillets
- Three medium sliced haddock fillets
- Two bay leaves
  - A quarter cup and two tablespoons of ghee
  - One cauliflower head, florets separated
  - Four eggs
  - Four cloves
  - One cup of whipping cream
  - Half cup of water
  - A pinch of nutmeg
  - One teaspoon of Dijon mustard
  - One and a half cup of shredded cheddar cheese
  - A handful of chopped parsley
  - Salt and black pepper as per taste
  - Four tablespoons of chopped chives

## Instructions

1. In a saucepan, place some water, add some salt, bring to a boil over medium heat, add the eggs, simmer for ten minutes, heat off, drain, cool, peel and break into quarters.
2. Place the water in another kettle, bring it to a boil, add the florets of cauliflower, simmer for 10 minutes, rinse, add a quarter of a cup of ghee, add it to the mixer, blend properly, and place it in a bowl.
3. Add the cream and half a cup of water to a saucepan, add the fish, toss and cover over medium heat.

4. Put to a boil, reduce heat to a minimum, and steam for 10 minutes. Put the cloves, onion, and bay leave.

5. Take the heat off, put the fish and set it aside in a baking dish.

6. Heat the saucepan with the fish, add the nutmeg, combine and simmer for 5 minutes.

7. Remove from the oven, discard the bay leaves and cloves and blend well with one cup of cheddar cheese and two tablespoons of ghee.

8. On top of the fish, set the egg quarters in the baking dish.

9. Sprinkle with cream and cheese sauce on top of the remaining cheddar cheese, chives and parsley, cover with cauliflower mash, sprinkle with the remaining cheddar cheese, and place in the oven for 30 minutes at 400 ° F.

10. Leave the pie until it is about to slice and serve, to cool down a little.

## 9.7 Lemon Dill Trout

Ready in about 20 minutes | Servings-4 | Difficulty-Easy

**Ingredients**

- Two pounds of pan-dressed trout (or other small fish), fresh or frozen
- One and a half teaspoons of salt
- A quarter teaspoon of pepper
- Half cup of butter or margarine
- Two tablespoons of dill weed
- Three tablespoons of lemon juice

**Instructions**

1. Cut fish lengthwise and season its inside with pepper and salt.

2. With melted butter and dill weed, prepare a frying pan.

3. For about two to three minutes per side, fry the fish flesh side down.

4. Remove the fish.

5. Add lemon juice to butter and dill to create a sauce.

6. Serve the fish and sauce together.

## 9.8 Sage N Orange Breast of Duck

Ready in about 20 minutes | Servings-4 | Difficulty-Easy

### Ingredients

- Six oz. Duck Breast (~6 oz.)

- Two tablespoons of Butter

- One tablespoon of Heavy Cream

- One tablespoon of Swerve

- Half teaspoon of Orange Extract

- A quarter teaspoon of Sage

- One cup of spinach

### Instructions

1. Score the duck skin on top of the breast and season with pepper and salt.

2. Brown butter in a saucepan over medium-low heat, and swerve.

3. Add the extract of sage and orange and cook until it is deep orangey in color.

4. Sear duck breasts for few minutes until nicely crunchy.

5. Flip the Breast of the Duck.

6. Add the orange and sage butter to the heavy cream and pour it over the duck.

7. Cook until finished.

8. In the pan that you used to make the sauce, add the spinach and serve with the duck.

## 9.9 Salmon with Caper Sauce

Ready in about 30 minutes | Servings-3 | Difficulty-Easy

### Ingredients

- Three salmon fillets
- Salt and black pepper as per taste
- One tablespoon of olive oil
- One tablespoon of Italian seasoning
- Two tablespoons of capers
- Three tablespoons of lemon juice
- Four minced garlic cloves
- Two tablespoons of ghee

### Instructions

1. Heat the olive oil pan over medium heat, add the skin of the fish fillets side by side, season with pepper salt and Italian seasoning, cook for two minutes, toss and cook for another two minutes, remove from heat, cover and leave aside for 15 minutes.
2. Put the fish on a plate and leave it aside.
3. Over medium heat, heat the same pan, add the capers, garlic and lemon juice, stir and cook for two minutes.
4. Remove the heat from the pan, add ghee and stir very well.
5. Put the fish back in the pan and toss with the sauce to coat.
6. Divide and serve on plates.

## 9.10 Bok Choy Stir Fry

Ready in about 20 minutes | Servings-2 | Difficulty-Easy

## Ingredients

- Two minced garlic cloves
- Two cups of chopped bok choy
- Two chopped bacon slices
- Salt and black pepper to the taste
- A drizzle of avocado oil

## Instructions

1. Heat a pan over medium heat with the oil, add the bacon, stir and brown until crunchy, move to paper towels and drain the oil.
2. Return the saucepan to medium heat, stir in the garlic and bok choy, and cook for 4 minutes.
3. Stir in salt, pepper and bacon, stir, cook for another 1 minute, divide among plates and serve.

# Chapter 10- Appetizer and Snacks Recipes

## 10.1 Cheeseburger Muffins

Ready in about 40 minutes | Servings-9 | Difficulty-Easy

### Ingredients

- Half cups of flaxseed meal

- Half cups of almond flour

- Salt and black pepper to the taste

- Two eggs

- One teaspoon of baking powder

- A quarter cups of sour cream

### For the filling

- Half teaspoons of onion powder

- Sixteen ounces of ground beef

- Salt and black pepper to the taste

- Two tablespoons of tomato paste

- Half teaspoons of garlic powder

- Half cups of grated cheddar cheese

- Two tablespoons of mustard

**Instructions**

1. Mix the almond flour with the flaxseed meal, pepper, salt and baking powder in a bowl and whisk together.

2. Add the sour cream and eggs and stir very well.

3. Divide it into a greased muffin pan and use your fingers to press well.

4. Over medium-high heat, heat a pan, add beef, stir and brown for a couple of minutes.

5. Stir well and add pepper, salt, garlic powder, onion powder and tomato paste.

6. Cook for an additional 5 minutes and take the heat off.

7. Fill the crusts with this mixture, place them in the oven at 350 degrees F and bake for fifteen minutes

8. Spread the cheese on top, put it in the oven again and cook the muffins for another 5 minutes.

9. Serve with mustard and your preferred toppings.

## 10.2 Pesto Crackers

Ready in about 30 minutes | Servings-6 | Difficulty-Easy

**Ingredients**

- Half teaspoons of baking powder

- Salt and black pepper to the taste

- One and a quarter cups of almond flour

- A quarter teaspoon of basil, dried

- One minced garlic clove

- Two tablespoons of basil pesto

- A pinch of cayenne pepper

- Three tablespoons of ghee

**Instructions**

1. Mix the pepper, salt, almond flour and baking powder together in a bowl.

2. Stir in the garlic, basil and cayenne.

3. Add whisk the pesto.

4. Also, add ghee and with your finger, mix your dough.

5. Spread this dough on a baking sheet and bake it at 325 degrees F in the oven for 17 minutes.

6. Leave your crackers aside to cool down, cut them and serve.

## 10.3 Tomato Tarts

Ready in about One hour and 20 minutes | Servings-4 | Difficulty-Easy

**Ingredients**

- A quarter cups of olive oil

- Two sliced tomatoes

- Salt and black pepper to the taste

**For the base**

- Five tablespoons of ghee
- One tablespoon psyllium husk
- Half cups of almond flour
- Two tablespoons of coconut flour
- A pinch of salt

## For the filling

- Two teaspoons of minced garlic
- Three teaspoons of chopped thyme
- Two tablespoons of olive oil
- Three ounces of crumbled goat cheese
- One small thinly sliced onion

## Instructions

1. On a lined baking sheet, spread the tomato slices, season with pepper and salt, drizzle with a quarter of a cup of olive oil, place in the oven at 425 degrees F and bake for 40 minutes.
2. Meanwhile, mix psyllium husk with almond flour, coconut flour, pepper, salt and cold butter in your food processor and stir until you've got your dough.
3. Divide this dough into cupcake molds of silicone, press well, place it in the oven at 350 degrees F and bake for 20 minutes.
4. Remove the cupcakes from the oven and leave them aside.
5. Also, take slices of tomatoes from the oven and cool them down a bit.
6. On top of the cupcakes, divide the tomato slices.

7. Heat a saucepan over medium-high heat with two tablespoons of olive oil, add the onion, stir and cook for 4 minutes.

8. Add the thyme and garlic, stir, cook for another 1 minute and remove from the heat.

9. Spread the mix over the tomato slices.

10. Sprinkle with the goat cheese, put it back in the oven and cook for five more minutes at 350 degrees F.

11. Arrange and serve on a platter.

## 10.4 Pepper Nachos

Ready in about 30 minutes | Servings-6 | Difficulty-Easy

### Ingredients

- One pound of halved mini bell peppers
- Salt and black pepper as per the taste
- One teaspoon of garlic powder
- One teaspoon of sweet paprika
- Half teaspoons of dried oregano
- A quarter teaspoon of red pepper flakes
- One pound of ground beef meat
- One and a half cups of shredded cheddar cheese
- One tablespoon of chili powder
- One teaspoon of ground cumin
- Half cups of chopped tomato
- Sour cream for serving

### Instructions

1. Mix the chili powder, pepper, salt, paprika, oregano, cumin, flakes of pepper and garlic powder in a bowl and stir.

2. Over medium heat, heat a pan, add beef, mix and brown for 10 minutes.

3. Add the mixture of chili powder, stir and take the heat off.

4. On a lined baking sheet, arrange the pepper halves, stuff them with the beef mix, sprinkle the cheese, place in the oven at 400 degrees F and cook for 10 minutes.

5. Remove the peppers from the oven, sprinkle with the tomatoes and divide among the plates and serve with sour cream.

## 10.5 Pumpkin Muffins
Ready in about One hour 25 minutes | Servings-18 | Difficulty-Easy

### Ingredients

- A quarter cups of sunflower seed butter
- 3/4 cups of pumpkin puree
- Two tablespoons of flaxseed meal
- A quarter cups of coconut flour
- Half cup of erythritol
- Half teaspoons of ground nutmeg
- one teaspoon of ground cinnamon
- Half teaspoons of baking soda
- One egg
- Half teaspoons of baking powder
- A pinch of salt

### Instructions

1. Mix the butter with the pumpkin puree and egg in a bowl and mix well.

2. Stir well and add coconut flour, flaxseed meal, erythritol, baking powder, baking soda, nutmeg, cinnamon and a pinch of salt.

3. Spoon this into an oiled muffin pan, add in the oven at 350 degrees F and cook for 15 minutes.

4. Let the muffins cool and serve them as a snack.

## 10.6 Fried Queso

Ready in about One hour 20 minutes | Servings-6 | Difficulty-Easy

**Ingredients**

- Two ounces of pitted and chopped olives,

- Five ounces of cubed and freeze queso Blanco

- A pinch of red pepper flakes

- One and a half tablespoons of olive oil

**Instructions**

1. Over medium-high heat, heat a pan with the oil, add cheese cubes and fry until the lower part melts a bit.

2. Flip the spatula cubes and sprinkle on top with black olives.

3. Let the cubes cook a little more, flip and sprinkle with the red flakes of pepper and cook until crispy.

4. Flip, cook until crispy on the other side, then move to a chopping board, cut into tiny blocks, and then serve.

## 10.7 Tortilla Chips

Ready in about 25 minutes | Servings-6 | Difficulty-Easy

**Ingredients**

## For the tortillas

- Two teaspoons of olive oil
- One cup of flaxseed meal
- Two tablespoons of psyllium husk powder
- A quarter teaspoon of xanthan gum
- One cup of water
- Half teaspoons of curry powder
- Three teaspoons of coconut flour

## For the chips

- Six flaxseed tortillas
- Salt and black pepper to the taste
- Three tablespoons of vegetable oil
- Fresh salsa for serving
- Sour cream for serving

## Instructions

1. Combine psyllium powder, flaxseed meal, xanthan gum, olive oil curry powder and water in a bowl and mix until an elastic dough is obtained.
2. On a working surface, spread coconut flour.
3. Divide the dough into six pieces, place each portion on the work surface, roll it into a circle and cut it into six pieces each.
4. Over medium-high heat, heat a pan with vegetable oil, add tortilla chips, cook on each side for 2 minutes and transfer to paper towels.
5. Put in a bowl of tortilla chips, season with pepper and salt and serve on the side with sour cream and fresh salsa.

## 10.8 Jalapeno Balls

Ready in about One hour 20 minutes | Servings-3 | Difficulty-Easy

### Ingredients

- Three slices of bacon
- Three ounces of cream cheese
- A quarter teaspoon of onion powder
- Salt and black pepper as per taste
- One chopped jalapeno pepper
- Half teaspoons of dried parsley
- A quarter teaspoon of garlic powder

### Instructions

1. Over medium-high heat, heat a skillet, add bacon, cook until crispy, switch to paper towels, remove the fat and crumble.
2. Reserve the pan's bacon fat.
3. Combine the jalapeno pepper, cream cheese, garlic powder and onion, parsley, pepper and salt in a bowl and stir thoroughly.
4. Use this blend to mix bacon crumbles and bacon fat, stir softly, form balls, and serve.

## 10.9 Maple and Pecan Bars

Ready in about 40 minutes | Servings-12 | Difficulty-Easy

### Ingredients

- Half cups of flaxseed meal
- two cups of pecans, toasted and crushed

- one cup of almond flour
- Half cups of coconut oil
- A quarter teaspoon of stevia
- Half cups of coconut, shredded
- A quarter cups of maple syrup
- **For the maple syrup**
- A quarter cups of erythritol
- Two and a quarter teaspoons of coconut oil
- One tablespoon of ghee
- A quarter teaspoon of xanthan gum
- 3/4 cups of water
- Two teaspoons of maple extract
- Half teaspoons of vanilla extract

## Instructions

1. Combine ghee with two and a quarter teaspoons of xanthan gum and coconut oil in a heat-proof bowl, stir, put in your oven and heat up for 1 minute.
2. Add the extract of erythritol, water, maple and vanilla, mix well and fire for 1 minute more in the microwave.
3. Mix the flaxseed meal and the coconut and almond flour in a bowl and stir.
4. Add the pecans, and stir them again.
5. Apply a quarter of a cup of maple syrup, stevia, and half a cup of coconut oil, and mix well.
6. Spread this in a baking dish, push well, position it at 350 degrees F in the oven and cook for 25 minutes.

7. To cool off, leave it aside, break into 12 bars and act as a keto snack.

## 10.10 Broccoli and Cheddar Biscuits

Ready in about One hour 35 minutes | Servings-12 | Difficulty-Easy

### Ingredients

- Four cups of broccoli florets

- One and a half cups of almond flour

- One teaspoon of paprika

- Salt and black pepper to the taste

- Two eggs

- A quarter cup of coconut oil

- Two cups of grated cheddar cheese

- One teaspoon of garlic powder

- Half teaspoons of apple cider vinegar

- Half teaspoons of baking soda

### Instructions

1. In your food processor, place the broccoli florets, add some pepper and salt and combine well.

2. Mix pepper, salt, paprika, baking soda and garlic powder with almond flour in a bowl and stir.

3. Apply the coconut oil, cheddar cheese, vinegar and eggs and stir.

4. Attach the broccoli and stir some more.

5. Shape Twelve patties, arrange them on a baking sheet, put them at 375 degrees F in the oven and bake for 20 minutes.

6. Switch the broiler in the oven and broil the biscuits for another 5 minutes.

7. Arrange and serve on a platter.

# Chapter 11- Dessert Recipes

## 11.1 Chocolate Truffles

Ready in about 20 minutes | Servings-22 | Difficulty-Easy

**Ingredients**

- One cup of sugar-free chocolate chips

- Two tablespoons of butter

- 2/3 cups of heavy cream

- Two teaspoons of brandy

- Two tablespoons of swerve

- A quarter teaspoon of vanilla extract

- Cocoa powder

**Instructions**

1. In a fire-proof mug, add heavy cream, swerve, chocolate chips and butter, stir, put in the microwave and heat for 1 minute.

2. Leave for 5 minutes, blend well, and combine with the vanilla and the brandy.

3. Stir again. Set aside for a few hours in the fridge.

4. Shape the truffles using a melon baller, cover them in cocoa powder and then serve them.

## 11.2 Keto Doughnuts

Ready in about 25 minutes | Servings-24 | Difficulty-Easy

### Ingredients

- A quarter cups of erythritol
- A quarter cups of flaxseed meal
- 3/4 cups of almond flour
- One teaspoon of baking powder
- One teaspoon of vanilla extract
- Two eggs
- Three tablespoons of coconut oil
- A quarter cups of coconut milk
- Twenty drops of red food coloring
- A pinch of salt
- One tablespoon of cocoa powder

### Instructions

1. Mix together the almond flour, cocoa powder, baking powder, erythritol and salt in a bowl and stir.

2. Mix the coconut oil with vanilla, coconut milk, food coloring and eggs in another bowl and stir.

3. Mix mixtures, use a hand mixer to stir, move to a bag, cut a hole in the bag and shape a baking sheet with 12 doughnuts.

4. Place it in the oven at 350 degrees F and cook for 15 minutes.

5. On a tray, place them and eat them.

## 11.3 Chocolate Bombs

Ready in about 20 minutes | Servings-12 | Difficulty-Easy

### Ingredients

- Ten tablespoons of coconut oil
- Three tablespoons of chopped macadamia nuts
- Two packets of stevia
- Five tablespoons of unsweetened coconut powder
- A pinch of salt

### Instructions

1. Place coconut oil in a casserole dish and melt over medium heat.
2. Apply stevia, salt and cocoa powder, mix well and remove from the heat.
3. Spoon this into a tray of candy and store it for a while in the freezer.
4. Sprinkle the macadamia nuts on top and hold them in the refrigerator until served.

## 11.4 Simple and Delicious Mousse

Ready in about 10 minutes | Servings-12 | Difficulty-Easy

### Ingredients

- Eight ounces of mascarpone cheese

- 3/4 teaspoons of vanilla stevia

- One cup of whipping cream

- Half-pint of blueberries

- Half-pint of strawberries

## Instructions

1. Combine the whipped cream with mascarpone and stevia in a cup and blend well with your mixer.

2. Assemble twelve glasses with a coating of strawberries and blueberries, then a layer of milk, and so on.

3. Serve cool.

## 11.5 Strawberry Pie

Ready in about 2 hours and 20 minutes | Servings-12 | Difficulty-Hard

## Ingredients

## For the filling

- One teaspoon of gelatin

- Eight ounces of cream cheese

- Four ounces of strawberries

- Two tablespoons of water

- Half tablespoon of lemon juice

- A quarter teaspoon of stevia

- Half cups of heavy cream

- Eight ounces of chopped strawberries for serving

- Sixteen ounces of heavy cream for serving

**For the crust**

- One cup of shredded coconut

- One cup of sunflower seeds

- A quarter cup of butter

- A pinch of salt

**Instructions**

1. Mix the sunflower seeds with coconut, butter and a pinch of salt in your food processor and stir well.

2. Place this in a greased springform pan and push the bottom well.

3. Heat a skillet over medium heat with the water, add gelatin, mix until it dissolves, remove the heat and leave to cool off.

4. Add it to your food processor, mix and blend well with 4 ounces of cream cheese, lemon juice, strawberries and stevia.

5. Stir well, pour half a cup of heavy cream and scatter over the crust.

6. Before slicing and serving, top with 8 ounces of strawberries and 16 ounces of heavy cream and keep in the refrigerator for 2 hours.

## 11.6 Keto Cheesecakes

Ready in about 25 minutes | Servings-9 | Difficulty-Easy

**Ingredients**

**For the cheesecakes**

- Two tablespoons of butter

- Eight ounces of cream cheese

- Three tablespoons of coffee
- Three eggs
- 1/3 cups of swerve
- One tablespoon of sugar-free caramel syrup

## For the frosting

- Three tablespoons of sugar-free caramel syrup
- Three tablespoons of butter
- Eight ounces of soft mascarpone cheese
- Two tablespoons of swerve

## Instructions

1. Combine eggs with cream cheese, two tablespoons butter, one tablespoon caramel syrup, coffee, and 1/3 cup swerve in your blender and pulse very well.

2. Spoon this into a pan of cupcakes, place it at 350 degrees F in the oven and cook for 15 minutes.

3. To cool down, leave aside and then keep in the freezer for three hours.

4. Meanwhile, mix three tablespoons butter with three tablespoons caramel syrup, two tablespoons swerve and mascarpone cheese in a bowl and mix well.

5. Spoon the cheesecakes over and serve them.

## 11.7 Peanut Butter Fudge

Ready in about 2 hours and 15 minutes | Servings-12 | Difficulty-Hard

## Ingredients

- One cup of unsweetened peanut butter

- A quarter cups of almond milk

- Two teaspoons of vanilla stevia

- One cup of coconut oil

- A pinch of salt

**For the topping**

- Two tablespoons of swerve

- Two tablespoons of melted coconut oil

- A quarter cups of cocoa powder

**Instructions**

1. Combine peanut butter with one cup of coconut oil in a heat-proof bowl, stir and heat in your microwave until it melts.

2. Add stevia, a pinch of salt and almond milk, mix it well and pour into a lined loaf pan.

3. Keep it for 2 hours in the refrigerator and then slice it.

4. Mix two tablespoons of cocoa powder and melted coconut in a bowl and swirl and stir well.

5. Drizzle over your peanut butter fudge with the sauce and serve.

## 11.8 Chocolate Pie

Ready in about 3 hours and 30 minutes | Servings-10 | Difficulty-Hard

**Ingredients**

**For the filling**

- One tablespoon vanilla extract

- Four tablespoons of sour cream

- One teaspoon of vanilla extract

- Four tablespoons of butter

- Sixteen ounces of cream cheese

- Half cup of cut stevia

- Two teaspoons of granulated stevia

- Half cup of cocoa powder

- One cup of whipping cream

## For crust

- Half teaspoons of baking powder

- One and a half cups of the almond crust

- A quarter cup of stevia

- A pinch of salt

- One egg

- One and a half teaspoons of vanilla extract

- Three tablespoons of butter

- One teaspoon of butter for the pan

## Instructions

1. With one teaspoon of butter, oil a springform pan and leave aside for now.

2. Mix the baking powder with a quarter cup of stevia, almond flour and a pinch of salt in a bowl and stir.

3. Add three tablespoons of butter, one teaspoon of egg, and one and a half teaspoons of vanilla extract, then mix till the time the dough is ready.

4. Press it well into the springform pan, place it at 375 degrees F in the oven and cook it for 11 minutes.

5. Take the pie crust out of the oven, cover it with tin foil and cook for another 8 minutes.

6. Take it out of the oven again and set it aside to cool down.

7. Meanwhile, add sour cream, four tablespoons of butter, one tablespoon of vanilla extract, half a cup of cocoa powder and stevia to the cream cheese in a bowl and mix it well.

8. Mix two teaspoons of stevia and one teaspoon of vanilla extract with the whipping cream in another bowl and stir using your mixer.

9. Combine two mixtures, pour into the pie crust, spread well, place for 3 hours in the refrigerator and serve.

## 11.9 Raspberry and Coconut Dessert
Ready in about 20 minutes | Servings-12 | Difficulty-Easy

**Ingredients**

- Half cup of coconut butter
- Half cup of coconut oil
- Half cup of dried raspberries
- A quarter cups of swerve
- Half cup of shredded coconut

**Instructions**

1. Mix the dried berries in your food processor very well.
2. Heat a pan over medium heat with the butter.
3. Stir in the coconut, oil and swerve, stir and cook for 5 minutes.

4. Pour half of this and spread well into a lined baking pan.

5. Add raspberry powder and also spread.

6. Spread the rest of the butter mix on top and keep it in the fridge for a while.

7. Cut and serve into pieces.

## 11.10 Vanilla Ice Cream

Ready in about 3 hours 20 minutes | Servings-6 | Difficulty-Hard

### Ingredients

- Four eggs, yolks and whites separated
- A quarter teaspoon of cream of tartar
- Half cups of swerve
- One tablespoon of vanilla extract
- One and a quarter cups of heavy whipping cream

### Instructions

1. Mix the egg whites with the tartar cream in a bowl and swerve and swirl using your mixer.

2. Whisk the cream with the vanilla extract in another bowl and mix thoroughly.

3. Combine and gently whisk the two mixtures.

4. Whisk the egg yolks very well in another bowl and then apply the combination of two egg whites.

5. Gently stir, put it into a container and leave it in the refrigerator for 3 hours until the ice cream is eaten.

# Chapter 12- Smoothie Recipes

## 12.1 Minted Iced Berry Sparkler

Ready in about 30 minutes | Servings-2 | Difficulty-Easy

**Ingredients**

- One cup of mixed frozen berries
- One lime or lemon
- One cup of fresh mint
- Twenty drops liquid Stevia extract (Clear / Berry)
- One large bottle of water
- Ice

**Instructions**

1. Wash the mint.

2. Cut the lime into wedges that are thin.

3. Using your option of sparkling or still water to put mint, frozen berries, lemon wedges or lime and leftover ingredients into all in a jar.

4. Let yourself relax for 15 minutes or more. The longer you keep it, the taste gets bolder.

5. Serve.

## 12.2 Body Pumping Smoothie

Ready in about 10 minutes | Servings-2 | Difficulty-Easy

### Ingredients

- One beetroot
- One Apple
- Three tablespoons of yogurt
- Handful of mint
- One thumb of a two-inch ginger
- Half teaspoon of black salt or rock salt
- One teaspoon of honey or sugar
- A quarter cup of water

### Instructions

1. Clean and remove the beet peel.
2. Slice the medium-sized apple and remove the nuts.
3. Add all the ingredients into the blender.
4. Add ice, then proceed to mix into a paste that is smooth.
5. Add juice from the lemon.
6. Enjoy and serve.

## 12.3 Kiwi Dream Blender

Ready in about 10 minutes | Servings-2 | Difficulty-Easy

### Ingredients

- A quarter average avocado
- One small wedge of Galia melon (or Honeydew, Cantaloupe)
- One scoop of vanilla whey protein powder (vanilla or plain)
- powdered gelatin
- Six drops liquid Stevia extract
- Ice as per the need
- A quarter cups of coconut milk (or coconut cream or full-fat cream)
- A quarter cup of kiwi berries or kiwi fruit
- One tablespoon of chia seeds (or psyllium)
- Half cups of water

### Instructions

1. Strip and peel the avocado and put it in a blender.
2. Add the kiwi, melon and the remaining ingredients to the flesh.
3. Blend until completely smooth.
4. Serve.

## 12.4 Keto Smart Banana Blender

Ready in about 10 minutes | Servings-2 | Difficulty-Easy

### Ingredients

- One cup of Spinach
- One cup of Banana

- Half cup of water and yogurt
- Two tablespoons of Pomegranate
- Two tablespoons of Almond meal/Almonds
- One teaspoon of Cinnamon powder
- One teaspoon of Vanilla sugar or Honey or Sugar and vanilla extract
- Ice

## Instructions

1. Clean the spinach and chop it coarsely.
2. Cut the Banana into medium-sized portions.
3. To make a half-cup of milk, blend two to three tablespoons of yogurt with water.
4. In a blender, mix all ingredients and process until smooth.
5. If the ideal thickness is met, add ice when blending.
6. Then serve.

## 12.5 Bright Morning Smoothie

Ready in about 15 minutes | Servings-2 | Difficulty-Easy

## Ingredients

- Two cups of Washed Spinach
- Two Large Strawberries
- A quarter cup of Lemon Juice or Fresh Squeezed Orange Juice
- Two tablespoons of Chia Seeds or Powder
- One cup of Green Tea
- One cup of Ice
- Four tablespoons of sweetener of choice

## Instructions

1. Place all of the ingredients in a mixer.

2. Blend it all until smooth.

3. Let it rest for about 5-10 minutes, then serve.

## 12.6 Keto Iced Strawberry and Greens
Ready in about 10 minutes | Servings-2 | Difficulty-Easy

## Ingredients

- Half cup coconut water

- One cup of ice

- One cup of washed spinach

- Three large strawberries

- Sweetener to taste

## Instructions

1. Blend all the ingredients together in a blender until smooth.

2. Let it rest for 5 minutes and then serve chilled.

## 12.7 Strawberry Lime Ginger Punch
Ready in about 10 minutes | Servings-2 | Difficulty-Easy

## Ingredients

- Two cups of water

- Two tablespoons of raw apple cider vinegar

- Three packets of NuStevia or any other sweetener

- Juice of one lime

- Half teaspoon of ginger powder

- Five frozen strawberries

## Instructions

1. Blend all the ingredients together in a blender until smooth.

2. Let it rest for 5 minutes and then serve chilled.

## 12.8 Mexican Comfort Cream

Ready in about 20 minutes | Servings-2 | Difficulty-Easy

## Ingredients

- Two handfuls of almonds blanched

- One cup of almond milk (unsweetened)

- One large egg

- Two tablespoons of whole or ground chia seeds

- One tablespoon of lime zest

- One teaspoon of cinnamon powder or one whole cinnamon stick

- Three tablespoons of erythritol or another healthy low-carb sweetener

- Twenty drops of liquid Stevia extract (Clear / Cinnamon)

- Two cups of warm water

## Instructions

1. Put in a bowl lime zest, the blanched almonds and cinnamon stick and cover with two teaspoons of hot water.

2. Let it rest for about eight hours or overnight.

3. Remove the lime zest and cinnamon stick after the almonds have been softened and put them in a shallow saucepan.

4. Mix almond milk. Purée until it's really smooth.

5. Steam the mixture and mix cinnamon and sweeteners before it begins to sizzle.

6. Whisk the egg when stirring constantly and pour it gently into the mixture.

7. Stir for a minute or two over the sun.

8. Remove from the heat and add in the seeds of chia.

9. To thicken the remainder.

10. Serve cold and pour in a bottle.

## 12.9 Strawberry Protein Smoothie

Ready in about 10 minutes | Servings-2 | Difficulty-Easy

### Ingredients

- Half cup water

- One cup of ice

- One scoop of strawberry protein powder

- One egg

- Two tablespoons of cream

- Two strawberries

### Instructions

1. Blend ice cubes and water together.

2. Apply the egg, powder and strawberries and start blending.

3. Pour in the cream.

4. Blend it again until smooth in a blender.

5. Serve and enjoy.

## 12.10 Low-Carb Caribbean Cream

Ready in about 2 hours and 10 minutes | Servings-1 | Difficulty-Moderate

### Ingredients

- Half cup of unsweetened coconut milk

- A quarter cups of coconut water or water (iced)

- One shot of dark or white rum

- One slice of fresh pineapple

- Five drops of liquid Stevia extract

## Instructions

1. In an ice cube tray, freeze the coconut water for 1-2 hours.

2. Blend coconut milk and pineapple until creamy.

3. Add the coconut water ice cubes and rum to the serving bottle.

4. Add the combined solution.

5. Use the pineapple to garnish.

6. Serve and enjoy.

# Keto diet Cookbook

## Best and easy diet to follow and maintain

## Alessandro Vasquez

# Table of Contents

# Introduction

We as human are all different, the effect of these eating systems can vary from one person to another but with several modifications to them so that they can suit you, there will only be benefits. Unfortunately, there are some individuals who should not attempt these fat loss regiments. If you have any severe health issues, it is mandatory to seek medical advice prior to beginning the new lifestyle, even if you are generally healthy, it is still advisable to consult a professional.

To clarify things even before diving right into the pool of data contained in this book, it is best to understand the difference between IF and the keto diet. IF is not a diet, but a meal planner that is designed to enhance weight loss and other health advantages, the keto diet is a diet that highly restricts carbohydrates and increases the amount of fat that you take so that you can be fuller for longer and be able to make fat your main energy source in the midst of other advantages that will be discussed later on.

The main reason why many doctors and nutritional experts give the "calories in-calories out" advice is that on paper it is simple and direct. They think that excessive calorie intake is the main cause of obesity; thus, the direct way of reversing this is consuming fewer calories. The 'eat less and move more' approach has been done for a very long time, and it simply does not work. The reason is that obesity and excessive weight gain is more of a hormonal imbalance than a calories imbalance. You will learn more about this and how the IF and the ketogenic diet can assist you in correcting this.

By reading this book, you will find a vast amount of information about IF and the ketogenic diet. You will know why and how they work so well and how they can work together to enhance your weight loss experience. You will also know about their benefits and downsides and how to be safe as you practice them.

During intermittent fasting, your body utilizes stubborn fat as it encourages metabolism that results in heat manufacture. This helps preserve muscle mass during weight loss and increases energy levels for keto dieters who want to lose weight and improve their athletic prowess. Combining the scheme of intermittent fasting and the ketogenic diet can lead to more body fat melting than individuals who follows IF but still consume junk food.

It can also increase your body structure as intermittent fasting improves human growth hormone output but at very large proportion. This hormone performs an enormous part in constructing muscles. The human growth hormone helps an individual reducing body fat concentrations and boost lean body and bone mass, according to studies conducted. Working out in a fasted state can result in metabolic adjustments in your muscle cells arising in energy fat burning. The human growth hormone also enables you to recover from injury or even difficult exercise at a quicker pace. It also decreases skin swelling.

The mixture of the two can even affect the aging process in a beneficial way. They cause the process of stem cells to rise. These are like construction blocks for the body as they can be transformed into any cell the body requires, as well as replacing ancient or harmed cells that keep you younger internally for longer. These stem cells can do wonders to old wounds, chronic pain, and much more. This can enhance your life expectaction as your general health is enhanced by balancing blood glucose, reducing swelling, and improving the free radical defense.

It can boost autophagy. This is simply cell cleaning measures. When it starts, your cells migrate through your inner components and remove any harmed or old cells and replace them with fresh ones. It's like an organ upgrade. It decreases inflammation and improves organ life.

There are no cravings, tiredness, and mood changes when exercising the ketogenic diet and intermittent fasting. This is accomplished through constantly small concentrations of blood sugar. This is because your blood sugar concentrations are not increased by fat. You will be prepared to keep small concentrations of blood sugar that can significantly assist individuals with Type 2 diabetes, even get off their drugs.

The liver transforms fat into packets of energy called ketones that are taken into the blood to offer your cells energy. These ketones destroy the ghrelin, the primary hunger hormone. High concentrations of ghrelin leave you famished while ketones decrease hormone concentrations even if your digestive tract does not contain any meals. This means you can stay without eating for a longer period of time and you won't get hungry. Undoubtedly, the ketogenic diet makes fasting much easier for you to do.

Some individuals follow the ketogenic diet integrated with intermittent fasting. This is by observing the ketogenic nutritional laws while also pursuing the trend of intermittent fasting eating. This can have many advantages, including high-fat burning levels, as both are important in using fats for energy over carbohydrates, providing you energy, reducing cholesterol in your body, controlling your blood sugar that can assist manage type 2 diabetes, helping to cope with hunger, and reducing skin inflammation.

For most individuals, combining the two is comfortable and can significantly speed up the fat burning process, making you accomplish your objectives quicker. However, one or the other can be done alone as they have many comparable advantages. Choosing an intermittent fasting unit that fits you is also essential and always makes sure you consume enough of the macro ingredients. Depending on what was in the meals, the functions can be comparatively fine for both. The job performed will be ideal when you mix both of them and will make weight loss much easier for you to do as both operate in distinct aspects but complement each other superbly.

## Successful stories

### 1. Actor.

John Cusack, the actor, is on a completely Keto diet and the majority of his life revolves around his Keto commitment. He is always seen doing physical activities with his wife, and their children. John admits to never ever getting sick. He follows a diet plan that has proven effective as seen from his movies. He is a big believer in the keto diet and the keto lifestyle.

You look good, where did you lose weight? Shusaku, the man in the center, did a diet that was popular in 2015. The year was 2015, and it was one of the worst years that American History would witness. John -John, the football player, hated tofu and chicken. He is a huge meat eater. That was why he implemented a Keto diet. It is a long-term diet, and it is relatively simple to follow. The kind of food you are going to eat will depend on your daily activity and the activity level on the day. The diet also depends on the activity and physical condition. There are those that enter the diet when they are sick. They do it because we feel good and we are looking good.

### 2. President Donald Trump.

Donald Trump wanted to lose weight. He was so overweight that he needed to take surgical precautions of his heart as he had developed heart problems. He is exploring various ways to take advantage of the positive effects of the Keto diet he is on. Trump was happy with the results that he was getting from the Keto diet. His heart surgeon had no choice but to say, "it is looking good. We are seeing the pounds melting off that boy." Trump said, "I am a believer in the Keto diet."

### 3. Kathryn Dennis.

Kathy says she has lost 60 pounds and that she hopes to do another 26-pound weight loss in the next year. She wants to get from 240 pounds to 119 pounds.

The girlfriend of professional football player Nate Washington says she went from a size 26 to a size 4, without taking shots of insulin. She decided to do the Keto diet in order to lose weight. She wanted to do the keto diet because of the weight loss, and the other benefits that the diet has to offer.

## 4. George W. Bush.

George Bush is a very avid Keto supporter. He has recently joined the Keto diet program and has gotten a lot of compliments and also a lot of medical advice. He started the Keto diet after he was diagnosed with coronary artery disease. His doctor told him to do away with food that has a high-fat content like meat and eggs, He was advised to fish, fruits, and vegetables and to do away with the high carb and fat drinks. He was advised to do away with all that has a high carbohydrate content. These include sugar, sugary drinks, potatoes, rice, pasta, and bread. As a result, he began to lose weight rapidly. He does not drink any high carb or fat meal. He does not like drinking any alcohol as he only drinks small quantities of beer once in a while. He can happily say he is enjoying his life on the Keto diet.

## 5. Shakira

Shakira is a singer. She is from Columbia, and she has Spanish ancestry. At a certain point in her life, she gave birth to her son, Milan. She gained a lot of weight because she wanted to nurse him. She could not give up on her baby. One day, she looked into the mirror, and she did not recognize herself. She realized that she was not happy. She researched on the Internet, and she came across the Keto diet. She went through it, and she did not move from step one to step two. She was determined to do everything properly. She followed what she was told to do, and she fully embraced the Keto lifestyle. She went on a diet with high fat, protein, and low carb content. She lost weight successfully.

## 6. Serena Williams.

Serena Williams is a tennis player. She is very successful. She is one of the best tennis players in the world, and she is primarily using the keto diet plan. She has been using the Keto diet because of her desire to lose weight. She does not eat any good that is high in carbs; she only eats vegetables, healthy food, fish, and meat. She consumes coconut oil, coconut milk, and salad dressings. She consumes something that has a high-fat content. She only eats one serving of carbs. This is a very good development for people that are trying to lose weight, and people that are trying to improve theirs constantly. Kick-off your new year by losing weight. You do not need a better reason to do it other than your desire to look good.

Eating is good for your health, and it keeps you healthy, but when you eat high-fat foods, and high carb foods, you could develop health problems, and you could get sick. What you want is to be healthy. When you are healthy, you are happy, and you can get new opportunities to be something you have always wanted to be.

# Recipes

## Almond Pancakes

Preparation:4 min
cooking:6 min
servings:

Ingredients:

- ½ cup almond flower

- ½ cup cream cheese

- 4 eggs

- Cinnamon to taste

- Truvia to taste/vanilla extract

- Sides:

- 3 eggs

- Sea salt and pepper to taste

- 1 tablespoon grass-fed butter

- ¼ cup sugar free syrup

Directions:

1. Mix all ingredients in a blender until smooth

2. Spray nonstick cooking spray in a medium pan, fry remaining 3 eggs, season with salt and pepper, cook to desire doneness

3. Enjoy your pancakes (2 pancakes are enough for a meal) with butter, syrup and eggs on the side.

*TIPS:* if you like, add some crunchy bacon

# Keto bread

Preparation:  6 min
cooking:50 min
servings:  6

Ingredients:

- 5 tablespoons of psyllium husk powder

- 1 ¼ cups almond flour

- 2 teaspoon baking powder

- 1 teaspoon sea salt

- 1 cup water

- 2 teaspoon cider vinegar

- 3 egg whites

- 2 tablespoon sesame seed if desired

Directions:

1. Preheat oven to 350 F

2. In a bowl mix all the dry ingredients

3. Bring the water to boil

4. Add vinegar and egg whites to the dry ingredients and combine well, add boiling water and mix for 30 seconds until you have the consistency of play-doh

5. Shape 6 rolls and put on the oven tray, top with sesame seeds if desired

6. Bake on lower rack for about 50-60 minutes.Serve with butter or toppings of your choice

# Jarlsberg Omelet

Preparation:  6 min

cooking:10 min

servings:1

Ingredients:

- 4 medium sliced mushrooms

- 2 oz. 1 green onion

- 1 tablesppon of butter sliced

- 2 eggs

- 1 oz Jarlsberg or Swiss cheese

- 2 slices of ham

Directions:

1. Cook the mushrooms the diced ham and the green onion in half of the butter in a big non-stick pan until the mushrooms are ready. Season with salt lightly, remove and set aside.

2. Melt over medium heat the remaining butter.

3. Add the beaten eggs

4. Now put the mushroom, ham and the grated cheese, on one side of the omelet.

5. Fold the plain side of the omelet over the filling once the eggs are almost ready.

6. Turn off the heat and leave until the cheese melts.

7. Enjoy it!

# Crockpot Southwestern Pork Stew

Preparation:10 min

cooking:  8 min

servings:4

Ingredients:

- 1 teaspoon of paprika

- 1 teaspoon of oregano

- 1/4 teaspoon of cinnamon

- 2 Bay leaf

- 6 oz. button mushrooms

- 1/2 Jalapeno

- 1 lb. sliced cooked pork shoulder

- 2 teaspoons Chili Powder

- 2 teaspoons cumin

- 1 teaspoon minced garlic

- 1/2 teaspoon Salt

- 1/2 teaspoon Pepper

- 1/2 Onion

- 1/2 Green Bell Pepper, chopped

- 1/2 Red Bell Pepper, chopped

- Juice from 1/2 Lime

- 2 cups bone broth

- 2 cups Chicken Broth

- 1/2 cup Strong Coffee

- 1/4 cup Tomato Paste

Directions:

1. Cut vegetables and stir fry on high heat in a pan. Once done, remove from heat.

2. Put sliced pork into the crockpot, add the mushrooms, bone broth, chicken broth, and coffee.

3. Add all the seasoning with the sauteed vegetables and stir well.

4. Cover the crockpot and cook for 4-10 hours at low temperature.

5. This recipe can be done with a cast iron boiler, the cooking time will be around 1 hour 20 minutes

# Pan-Roasted Rib Eye Steak with Pan Jus

Preparation:45 min
cooking:20 min
servings:  3

Ingredients:

- 1 (1 pound) rib-eye steak

- 4 spoons of olive oil

- 1/2 cup Chicken Broth

- 3 spoons of room temperature butter

- sea salt and pepper to taste

Directions:

1. Before cooking, remove steak from the fridge for about 45 minutes, pat it dry, and salt it completely. Flip it through for about 20 minutes, remembering when flipping to pat it dry, and then again before cooking.

2. If you want to cook your steak medium or medium-well, preheat your oven to 200 ° F. Heat on the stovetop a cast-iron skillet or another pan over elevated heat.

3. Add the oil to the casserole.

4. Place the meat in the pan just before it starts smoking, then listen to the searing sound.

5. Leave it to cook for 3 to 5 minutes without shifting it.

6. Once the bottom has a pleasant brown color (you can check by lifting one edge of the steak to look at the bottom) flip over the steak and do the same on the other.

7. This will offer you a steak that is medium-rare. If you want to continue cooking, place medium-well in the oven at 200 ° F for 5 to 6 minutes and medium-well for 7 to 8 minutes.

8. Once done, put it on a cutting board for 5 minutes to rest.

9. Slice it and serve it.

10. Make the pan jus while the meat rests.

11. Transfer the pan to the stovetop, add the broth and water over medium heat, reduce the sauce by half, add the butter and stir from 2 to 4 minutes.

12. Pour the Jus over the meat and enjoy.

# Conclusion

The ketogenic diet comprises a low-carbohydrate, high-protein and high-fat diet with a lengthy history of use in the management of intractable childhood seizures. Amid the existence of growing quantities of modern antiepileptic medications and surgical therapies, this nutritional therapy has enjoyed increasing success in recent years.

The authors study the past of the ketogenic diet, its conventional initiation protocol, potential modes of operation, proof of success, and side effects. In particular, several of the fields of an ongoing study in this area are illustrated, as are potential paths and unresolved issues.

An efficient and reasonably healthy cure for intractable epilepsy is the ketogenic diet. However, considering its lengthy past, everything regarding the diet, including its modes of operation, the optimum protocol, and the complete extent of its applicability, remains unclear. Diet study offers fresh insight into the causes underlying epilepsy and seizures itself, as well as potential possible approaches.

It would not be unreasonable to claim that when it comes to intermittent fasting, there is little to fear. While at first, you will feel starving, by triggering autophagy and losing more fat and ketones for food, your body will adapt.

A longer intermittent fast accompanied by shorter regular intermittent fasts is proposed by ketogenic diet researchers. In the days preceding and during the three-day fast, you will use a fasting regimen that involves fasting for up to three days, 3 to 4 times a year, with a shorter 10 to 18 hour fast.

If you are fasting for sixteen hours or three days to prevent symptoms of refeeding syndrome, checking your mineral levels is crucial.

To prevent unnecessary mineral depletion induced by ketogenic diets and fasting, supplementation of sodium from unprocessed potassium and salt, phosphate, and magnesium from mineral-rich foods or supplements could be essential.

To put an end to it, it won't be wrong to say that the Ketogenic Diet is a miraculous diet as it focuses on healthy starvation and lets the body utilize the already stored fat and fastens the weight loss procedure as the intake of calories is less and the already stored fat is converted into energy by the body.

Lightning Source UK Ltd.
Milton Keynes UK
UKHW052004060821
388460UK00005B/509

9 781803 573250